Beyond Desert Storm

Hope For The Days Ahead

Norman W. Mathers

This publication is designed to provide accurate and authoritative information in regard to the subject matter covered. It is sold with the understanding that the publisher is not engaged in rendering legal, accounting, or other professional service. If legal advice or other assistance is required, the services of a competent professional person should be sought. From a Declaration of Principles jointly adopted by a Committee of the American Bar Association and a Committee of Publishers.

Library of Congress Cataloging-in-Publication Data

Mathers, Norman W.,
    Beyond Desert Storm / by Norman W. Mathers.
    p. cm.
    ISBN 0–9634654–0–6 (paper) : $9.95
    1. Bible—Prophecies—Middle East. 2. Armageddon.
    I. Title.
BS649.N45M38   1992   92–59967
236′.9—dc20   CIP

Manufactured in the United States of America
AGF-PA
987654321

Introduction

The Middle East is without a workable peace plan. What does this mean for the Jew, the Arab and you? The recent Gulf Crisis and Operation Desert Storm proved the crisis in the Middle East is no longer a regional conflict.

The problem of the Middle East could explode all the world. During the recent Gulf Crisis - we asked: "Are we approaching Armageddon?" The superpowers responded to the threat of possible global destruction. The Crisis subsided! No peace plan came about. The peace initiative for the region failed. Why is a peace treaty that guarantees peace and security in the region not possible?

Beyond Desert Storm was written to address the new questions that the Gulf Crisis had raised. What are we to make of the Arab rhetoric of Land for Peace? The Israeli response that the real question is their existence. *Beyond Desert Storm* explores the complications for the Arab, the Jew and the rest of the world. The question of nuclear weapons, Iraq, the new Israeli mood, and Arab doctrine, are developed from the number one best seller and as necessary from history and philosophy.

The Bible predicts Desert Storm II, and then Armageddon, are we the generation? Will the next Middle East crisis lead to Armageddon? Iraq and Russia - what part will they play? How will Israel meet the challenge? Life in the West - hard, easy, uncertain or annihilation? Is it a nuclear war? *Beyond Desert Storm* was written to answer your questions and bring you hope for the days ahead.

The study of the Bible on these subjects reveals an Armageddon Context, Chronology and Calendar of events. When the days ahead are studied a natural order of the sequence of events can be formed. It seems reasonable to

3

present the logical deductions that can be made that we might have hope and direction for the future.

Beyond Desert Storm is not a topical presentation of some topics to the exclusion of other important subjects. In *Beyond Desert Storm*, each chapter is developed in a consecutive fashion so that the next chapter begins where the previous left off.

The logical place to begin is the unsolvable human problem the peace plan of the Middle East. This thought provoking work on the subject of future things is written using a philosophical method. Sound theological content is woven within a framework of philosophical deductions.

My qualifications are excellent for writing such a work both by education and my experience. I have taught the subject of future things to groups of all ages. The last few years have found the same content communicated to students both at the College and Seminary level. I have two earned Master's degrees a Th.M. from Dallas Theological Seminary which afforded me the comprehensive content that other well known teachers received. The M.A. degree from California State University, Carson, California in Humanities - Philosophy and Religion helped me develop the skills of critical thinking. I have an earned Ph.D. degree from Columbia Pacific University, San Rafael, California. I have been able to develop the material perhaps more fully than most Bible expositors are able to do because many authors on the subject do not possess an earned M.A. and Ph.D. They have not acquired the necessary rational skills to develop the material beyond the level of a Bible exposition presentation for their reading audience.

Study questions for individuals and groups form an essential part of each chapter.

I hope that the non-Christian will find some of their questions answered. My prayer is that the Christian will be edified and blessed and comforted by the hope that *Beyond Desert Storm* will bring to their soul.

Contents

Dedication

To Norma and our four gifts:
Robert
Ruthlyn
Rachel
Victoria Grace

1
The Unsolvable Human Problem

Saddam Hussein Like Individual - This One Succeeds

The prophecy of Daniel chapter seven reveals the solution to the Middle East Crisis. The vision was given to Daniel who was a captive then in Babylon. (Iraq) Daniel said, "I was looking in my vision by night, and behold, the four winds of heaven were stirring up the sea the great one" (Dan. 7:2). We have a picture of heaven controlling and determining the earth's history. The Bible presents to us the course of Gentile world history. Chapter seven is parallel to chapter two which reveals five world empires Babylon (Iraq), Medo-Persia (Iran), Greece, and Rome and then a Revived Roman Empire. The book of Daniel was recorded by Daniel the Jewish youth in the sixth century B.C. Conservative scholarship has refuted the liberal ideas that Daniel was written down after the events had taken place. Daniel described the Roman Empire in 7:7: "After this I kept looking in the night visions and behold, a fourth beast, dreadful and terrifying and extremely strong; and it had large iron teeth. It devoured and crushed, and trampled down the remainder with its feet, and it was different from all the beasts that were before it, and had ten horns." Yet Daniel focuses on the little horn that comes out of the Roman Empire (Dan. 7:8). "While I was contemplating the horns, behold, another horn, a little one, came up among them, and the three of the first

7

horns were pulled out by the roots before it; and behold, the horn possessed eyes like the eyes of a man, and a mouth uttering great boasts."

The action shifts to heaven where the court of heaven sits in judgment on this dictator. "I kept looking until thrones were set up, and the Ancient of Days took His seat; The court sat, and the books were opened" (Daniel 7:9-10). The little horn is interpreted for us in Daniel 7:20 & 24: "and the meaning of the ten horns that were on its head, and the other horn which came up, and before which three of them fell, namely, that horn which had eyes and a mouth uttering great boasts, and which was larger in appearance than its associates." "As for the ten horns, out of the kingdom ten kings will arise; and another will arise after them, and he will be different from the previous ones and will subdue three kings." The dictator is a King supported by a ten nation confederacy. A dictator backed by ten nations is a current idea in our modern world. The ten kings will arise out of the Old Roman Empire (Dan. 7:23). Daniel 7:24 pinpoints the fact that the ten kings come "out of this kingdom." This idea of a king being backed by another King or a series of Kings is as old as Biblical times and as modern as our contemporary century.

The importance of this dictator is emphasized by the Law of Literary proportion and a repeated theme throughout the book of Daniel. Daniel eight describes the 8th Syrian King of the line of Seleucus 175-164 B.C. This one Antiochus Epiphanes "Antiochus the Madman" foreshadows our dictator.

Daniel 9 picks up the theme of the dictator in 9:26, and 9:27. In Daniel 11:36-45, the Bible describes him as a military dictator who worships the god of military might. Saddam Hussein, in our day, is as well another type of Antiochus who foreshadows the world dictator the AntiChrist. The New Testament gives great importance to this world dictator who is yet to come from Matthew to the apocalyptic literature of the book of the Revelation. The

8

Lord Jesus spoke of the dictator in Mt. 24:15, "Therefore when you see the Abomination of Desolation which was spoken of through Daniel the prophet, standing in the holy place (let the reader understand)." Satan (adversary) when tempting the Lord Jesus, made reference to the dictator, "And the devil (slanderer) said to Him, I will give you all this domain and its glory: for it has been handed over to me, and I will give it to whomever I will" (Lk. 4:6). The Lord Jesus referred to the dictator in John 5:43, "I have come in my Father's name, and you do not receive Me; if another shall come in his own name, you will receive him." While Israel rejected Christ yet the Lord Jesus refers to the fact that the nation will accept the dictator as Messiah. Paul the apostle stresses the importance of the dictator in 2 Thess. 2:3, "that no one in any way deceive you, for it will not come unless the apostasy comes first, and the man of lawlessness is revealed, the Son of Destruction."

The apostle gives us extensive new revelation concerning the dictator. The false prince of peace is called the "man of lawlessness" and "the son of destruction." He is the one who demands to be worshiped as God, "who opposes and exalts himself above every so-called god or object or worship, so that he takes his seat in the temple of God, displaying himself as God (2 Thess. 2:4). The whole question of the dictator has to do with the mystery of lawlessness. This continuing increase in lawlessness results in the revealing of the Man of Sin (2 Thess. 2:7).

The Man Of Sin

Lawlessness spreads and is rampant by divine permission. It comes to fruition and fullness in the Man of Sin. "For the mystery of lawlessness is already at work, only he who restrains will do so until he is taken out of the way" (2 Thess. 2:7). The Spirit of God is the restrainer holding back the complete tide of evil so that total lawlessness and chaos and confusion do not prevail upon the earth. When we hear of the dastardly deeds that are

9

committed throughout the earth which are altogether lawless acts then let us remember that the mystery of lawlessness is at work. The rapture must come first "then that lawless one will be revealed." The first judgment of God on the world as outlined in the apocalyptic literature of Revelation chapter 6 is the false prince of peace. "And I looked, and behold, a white horse, and he who sat on it had a bow; and he went out conquering, and to conquer" (Rev. 6:2). The Bible predicts: "Let no one deceive you, for it will not come unless the apostasy comes first, and the man of lawlessness be revealed the son of destruction" (2 Thess. 2:3). The English word apostasy is the Greek word apostasia transliterated without any English meaning. The usage of the word in the book of Acts is always that of departure. The word apostasy is used in Acts 21:21 of a departure from the Law of Moses. "And they have been told about you, that you are teaching all the Jews who are among the Gentiles to forsake Moses, telling them not to circumcise their children nor to walk according to the customs (Acts 21:21).

Lawlessness Spreads

Thus the world is becoming an increasingly disorderly and chaotic place as the mystery of iniquity continues to develop coming eventually to fruition in the Man of Sin (2 Thess. 2:7). The Spirit of God is the restrainer of the tide of evil so that total lawlessness and chaos and confusion do not prevail upon the earth. As we continue to hear of the deeds that are continually committed throughout the earth then let us remember that the mystery of lawlessness is at work. The rapture must come first "then that lawless one will be revealed" after the catching up and out of this world of the blood bought company of believers. The first judgment of God on the world outlined in the apocalyptic literature of Revelation chapter 6 is the false prince of peace. "And I looked, and behold, a white horse, and he who sat on it had a bow; and he went out conquering, and to conquer" (Rev. 6:2).

The Bible predicts: "Let no one deceive you, for it will not come unless the apostasy comes first, and the man of lawlessness be revealed the son of destruction" (2 Thess. 2:3). The Scriptures tell us at great length of this world dictator. Revelation chapters 12, 13; 17 and 19 explain further the reign of the "beast." How long will this evil dictator rule upon the earth? This Hitler-Hussein-like individual will rule for seven years upon the earth. He will exercise a complete religious, military, socio-economic control over the Western world and the Middle East. He will succeed where others have failed. The dictator's reign begins after the Rapture of the Church has taken place first. In 2 Thess. 2:3, "the departure comes first, and the man of lawlessness is revealed." The reign of the AntiChrist is tied to the working of God with the nation Israel as found in Daniel 9:27. "And he will make a firm covenant with the many for one week (heptad). The heptad is a unit of seven for the Jew who counted by sevens not ten as the base of their number system. The final seven year period whereby God will finish His prophetic program for Israel begins with the dictator making a peace treaty with Israel. The context of Daniel chapters 8 to 12 deal with the divine decree of God to complete his prophetic plan for the nation Israel. "Seventy weeks (70x's 7 = 490 years) have been decreed for your people and your holy city, to finish the transgression, and to make an end of sin, "to make atonement for iniquity, to bring in everlasting righteousness, to seal up vision and prophecy, and to anoint the most holy place" (Dan. 9:24). Jerusalem is specifically mentioned in Daniel 9:25 so that the prophet statesman Daniel is receiving truth about His people Israel. Daniel is praying about his people in their captivity in Babylon (Iraq). "Indeed all Israel has transgressed Thy law and turned aside, not obeying Thy voice; so the curse has been poured out on us, along with the oath which is written in the law of Moses the servant of God, for we have sinned against Him" (Dan. 9:11).

The Peace Treaty

"And he will make a covenant with the many for one week, but in the middle of the week he will put a stop to sacrifice and grain offering: and on the wing of abominations will come one who makes desolate, even until a complete destruction, one that is decreed, is poured out on the one who makes desolate." (Dan. 9:27) Our world represented by the super powers has been trying for the past ten years to bring Israel to the peace table with her Arab neighbors. The Bible predicts that although the world has stumbled upon the right means the peace treaty idea yet it will only succeed as presented by the dictator. The peace treaty will give guaranteed security to Israel within her land. Ezekiel who received much revelation from God as did Daniel during the Babylonian captivity has written: "After many days you will be summoned: (the prophet speaks of Russia and her allies) in the latter years you will come into the land that is restored from the sword, whose inhabitants have been gathered from many nations to the mountains of Israel which had been a continual waste; but its people were brought out from the nations, and they are living securely, all of them." (Ezekiel 38:8) The Lord God declares: "It will come about on that day, that thoughts will come into your mind, and you will devise an evil plan, and you will say, I will go up against those who are at rest, that live securely, all of them living without walls, and having no bars or gates." (Ezek. 38:11)

What Have We Said?

In the preceding passages, the Bible makes two very important points for one to be able to understand the prophetic timetable of the Lord God Almighty. First, extensive revelation is given in the Old and New Testaments to the coming world dictator's rule of seven years. Secondly, Israel makes a peace treaty with this individual the world dictator who guarantees her a false peace.

Rainbows

The Rainbow is a very popular symbol today in our modern world. In the book of the Revelation, the last book in the Bible, the rainbow is a symbol of the false peace that AntiChrist is to bring to our world. The Rainbow will symbolize as well the world citizens who are for the World Dictator. Thus whenever we see the symbol of the rainbow on cars in back windows or on bumpers, they represent the conditioning process that is taking place from a purely psychological perspective. Nevertheless, it is happening in our day to day world, people are ready to trade their country, their national spirit in many cases unfortunately for their own peace and personal security.

John writes in Revelation 6:1: "And I looked, and behold, A White Horse, and He who sat on it had a bow; and a crown was given to him; and he went out conquering, and to conquer."

World Leader Pretends
Submission to World Church

The world leader makes a peace treaty with Israel according to Daniel 9:27 at the beginning of the world's last seven years of history. Yet according to the New Testament Revelation chapter 17:3, the world's ecumenical church controls the dictator initially: "and he carried me away in the Spirit into a wilderness; and I saw a woman sitting on a scarlet boast, full of blasphemous names, having seven heads and ten horns." The woman a figure of speech dressed in the colors of the church Revelation chapter 17:4,5 is described for us: "Here is the mind which has wisdom. The seven heads are seven mountains on which the woman's sit." The common geographical description is well known to be Rome!

The Woman's authority is over many "peoples and multitudes and nations and tongues." (Revelation 17:5) We have before us a very interesting point from the perspective of not only Scripture but church history.

Protestantism is reabsorbed back into the Roman Catholic Church. The world ecumenical super church is according to the Scripture to be destroyed by the world dictator. The Roman Catholic Church which reabsorbed the Protestant church is destroyed by the world dictator. (Rev. 17:16-17)

World Leader Supported
By World Religious Leader

Initially, the world dictator is given "his power and his throne and great authority" by the Devil. (Rev. 13:2) The world follows the dictator as their leader for the first three and a half years while the earth is given to the worship of the Devil. The Bible says: "and they worshiped the dragon because he gave his authority to the beast; and they worshiped the beast saying, "Who is like the beast, and who is able to wage war with him"? (Rev. 13:4) The actual worship of the Devil and the Anti-Christ is during the three and a half years of the Great Tribulation.

The world leader will be a Gentile according to Revelation 13:1: "I saw a beast coming out of the sea having ten horns and seven heads." The sea in Scripture is largely used as a figure for the Gentile nations. The entrance of the beast to a world political leadership and a world wide following is the result of his coming back to life from death. (Rev. 13:13-14) "And the whole earth was amazed and followed after the beast."

The world religious figure gives his support to the world leader. (Rev. 13:11-18) The prophet-beast performs signs by all the power and authority of the dragon. (Rev. 13:11) The dragon in the book of the Revelation is clearly outlined to be the Devil. Devil is translated with the English meaning of slanderer both of man and God. It will be wonderful one day when the Devil is bound for the thousand years. (Rev. 20:2) This thousand year binding of Satan will take place during the millennial kingdom. The Scriptures assign clearly the description of the dragon to be the Devil. The Devil is taught in the Bible to be a person. He is a fallen and corrupted cherubim. Secondly, the false prophet makes a statue of the world leader come to life. (Rev. 13:15)

Religious Deception- World Wide

The religious prophet's ministry by divine permission gives way to world wide religious deception. His message is that the first beast (the world dictator) is God. (Rev. 13:15) The apostle Paul in 2 Thess. 2:11-12 predicts the world's reception of the false prophet's ministry: "and for this reason God will send them a deluding influence so that they may be damned who did not believe the truth, but took pleasure in wickedness." The citizens of the world believed the lie the world dictator is God. The deluding and deceiving influence is the world wide ministry of the false prophet. Those who did believe the lie wanted to because they loved the pleasure of unrighteousness which the Lord God of heaven had forbidden. Unrighteousness is outlined for us in Romans 1:28-32. The dictator claimed to be God. The false prophet proclaims this message throughout the earth. The world is given to the worship of the dictator. The worship of the beast is seen by a mark on their right hand or on their forehead. The prophet's ministry is to identify all those who belong to the beast. The prophet enforces that no one can live without the mark of the beast dictator. If they cannot buy nor sell then starvation, bankruptcy and death are certain. World dictatorship would certainly mean the end of the free market and all private assets to the world dictator. Remember the false promise of the false peace by the symbol of the Rainbow.

Seventy Weeks

Daniel chapter nine reveals to us the divine plan for Israel. The prophet-statesman was taken captive to Babylon as a teenager living there for some seventy years. The captivity (the Babylonian exile) is about up at the time of the 9th chapter of the prophecy. The background for this chapter in Daniel is Deuteronomy chapter 30 where the Palestinian covenant is to be found. Daniel understood that God had promised to lift the discipline if the nation repented and turned to him with all their heart. (Deut. 30:1-3)

I, Daniel Observed

The prophet was meditating upon the book of Jeremiah concerning the completion of the captivity and the return to Jerusalem for Daniel's people. (Dan. 9:2) The prophecy from Jeremiah is found in Jeremiah 25:11-12 which formed part of Daniel's devotions. In Daniel 9:3-9, we have the divine pattern for prayer. (Confession-9:5-14, Petition 9:15-19, based on Scripture) Daniel prayed back the Scriptures to the Lord God reminding Him of that which He had written for Israel.

God's Righteous Character

Now Daniel reminds the Lord God that having confessed his sin and the sin of the nation, it would be in line with God's righteous character to lift the discipline. (Dan. 9:16-19) Daniel reminded the Lord God that His Name was at stake. Daniel's prayer was based on his knowledge of God's great compassion. God is the God of all compassion. We read so often in the New Testament that the Lord Jesus was moved with compassion.

Gabriel Informs Daniel

God answered and the word went out that which was the revealed will of God based on His Eternal Decree for Jerusalem. The command of Daniel 9:23 was the mission to send Gabriel to inform Daniel of the plan of God for the nation and the holy city Jerusalem. (Dan. 9:24-27)

The Plan

The divine plan or decree of God to complete His prophetic program encompasses 490 years for the nation Israel. The word translated week is the Hebrew word heptad. The heptad was a period of seven years as illustrated for us in Genesis 29:27-30. Jacob served Laban seven-years for Leah and another seven years for Rachel. The Hebrew mind thought in terms of seven rather than as we do ten being the basis for the Roman number system. Given one heptad is equal to seven years then seventy weeks (heptads) is equal to four hundred and ninety years. (Dan. 9:24) The time span was "to finish the transgression, to make an end of sin, to make atonement for iniquity." The first set of three phrases has to do with the Redeeming work of Messiah Jesus Christ at His First Advent. The second set of three phrases has to do with bringing in "everlasting righteousness, to seal up vision and prophecy, and to anoint the most holy place." These deal with the establishment of Christ's millennial kingdom on the earth and the fulfillment of the Jewish covenants the Abrahamic, the Palestinian, the Davidic and the New. Included within this great scope of promise is the establishment of the incomparable millennial temple on the earth during the millennium. (Dan. 9:24)

The Decree To Rebuild Jerusalem

The prophetic word points further that from the issuing of the decree to restore and rebuild Jerusalem until Messiah the prince there will be seven weeks and sixty-two weeks. The decree revealed to Daniel by Gabriel is found in Nehemiah 2:5-8. The date historically is March 14, 445 B.C. Seven weeks (heptads) times seven equals 49 years until Jerusalem was to be rebuilt. Sixty-two weeks (heptads) times seven would equal 434 years until Messiah Jesus Christ would present himself to the nation. Daniel 9:26 makes clear to us that after 62 heptads that Messiah will be cut off. The Savior Jesus Christ was crucified in April 32 A.D. The Word of God tells us once Messiah was crucified "the people of the prince who is to come will destroy the city and the sanctuary." (Dan. 9:26) The temple and the city of Jerusalem was destroyed by the Romans in 70 A.D. Once Daniel 9:24-26 had been completed only one week of the total 70 weeks (heptads) that is one seven year period is left on God's prophetic time clock.

The Clock Is Stopped

God's clock has stopped between the 69th week and the 70th week. According to Daniel 9:27, the final seven year period is yet future: "And he will make a firm covenant with the many for one week." The "he" refers back to the "people of the prince who is to come." The Anti-Christ is to be a descendant out of the Roman Empire in it's revived form. The world dictator as predicted in Daniel 9:27 will make a peace treaty with the nation Israel. He will protect Israel for the first three and a half years of this final seven year period. However, at the mid-point of this final seven year, he the dictator will become a terrible persecutor of the nation. (Dan. 9:27)

This is the reason that a lasting peace treaty in the Middle East is not possible between the Arabs and the Jews at present. This is reserved for Anti-Christ and the world church to make a peace treaty with Israel bringing a comprehensive yet not an everlasting peace to the region. The present peace initiatives fail. The reason is that the eternal decree of God has determined this to come about at the beginning of the last week (heptad equals seven years) on God's prophetic time clock. Is it any wonder that modern man's peace attempts fail?

Yes, Israel Will Be Persecuted

The predictions of the peace treaty, the reign of the dictator, and the persecution of Israel are still future. How do we know that this is true? The same prediction was future in Jesus day as seen in Matthew 24:15 and no such event has ever happened. The reign of a world dictator has not been known since the days of the Roman Emperor in the Roman Empire. Although the Roman Emperors are not given this status in the Scriptures as a type of Anti-Christ. The prophetic time clock for the nation Israel that stopped at the fulfillment of the 69th week when Christ entered Jerusalem on Palm Sunday will begin to tick. The clock will start again and those on the earth will know when Anti-Christ and the world church bring about a comprehensive peace plan with Israel. The very talk of our world today is for a peace plan for the Middle East. (Dan. 9:27, Luke 19:42)

What does Daniel 9 teach about these themes so relevant and so troubling to our modern world? The Middle East conflict of the future like the past crisis in the Gulf will draw the whole world into an international arena of conflict. No nation or people will escape that terrible hour that seven year period of trouble to come on the earth. Only the church which is caught up before the Tribulation begins will escape the coming Wrath of God. (I Thess. 5:1-11) The Middle East dictator's settlement of the conflict in the region will be temporal for at the mid-point of the final seven years, he will become a persecutor of Israel. (Daniel 9:27)

Chapter One Study Questions

1. What does Daniel chapters 2 and 7 tell us about the nations of the world?

2. Who is the little horn?

3. What is the mystery of lawlessness referred to in II Thessalonians chapter 2?

4. How is a comprehensive peace plan possible for the Middle East?

5. When does God's prophetic time clock begin to tick again?

Challenge Questions

1. Who supports the little horn?

2. What relationship comes to pass between Israel, the beast, the false prophet, and the world church?

• • • • •

2
Child Of Wrath

Jesus Christ Ready To Judge

Jesus who was crucified and rose from the dead is presented to us in the first chapter of the Book of Revelation set to judge the earth, both Israel and the Nations.

Heaven Judges The Earth

John the Apostle saw the throne and the "One sitting on the throne." (Rev. 4:2) The brilliance of the Father as the Glory of God emanates from His person is compared to light shining through precious stones. (Rev. 4:3) All of heaven the redeemed elders, the cherubim and the seraphim worship, proclaim and protect the Holiness of God. (Rev. 4:4-9) Listen to what heaven is saying: "And when the living creatures give glory and honor and thanks to Him....who lives forever and ever....Worthy art Thou our Lord and our God, to receive glory and honor and power; for Thou didst create all things, and because of Thy will they were created." (Rev. 4:9-11) All of heaven proclaims God's Sovereign Right over the Earth to Judge it because He has created it. All of heaven falls in worship and in adoration of God the Father's right to rule over and upon the earth.

Heaven worships Jesus Christ! Chapter 5 of the book of Revelation reveals to us the glorified God man in heaven Jesus Christ and the judgment program of God. (Rev. 5:1-4) Jesus Christ is praised by heaven for redeeming men. (Rev. 5:9) He alone is able to take the book with it's seals from the Father.

Jesus alone is worthy since He has paid the ultimate price for the world's redemption His blood. Yet the Bible declares as well that Christ died for the elect. (Rom. 8:33-34) The application of the death of Christ to the sinner is the only acceptable basis of forgiveness with God the Father. Judgment Comes!

God the Father moves in readiness to judge the earth! The first judgment of God upon the earth is to deliver the world into the hands of Anti-Christ. (Rev. 6:3-4) "And I looked, and behold, a white horse, and he who sat on it had a bow; and a crown was given to him; and he went out conquering and to conquer." The breaking of the second seal results in war upon the earth! (Rev. 6:3) Peace is taken from the earth and men slay one another. Here is one of the paradoxes of the Bible, the white horse interpreted as Anti-Christ has the "bow" the false symbol of peace which brought a temporary peace to the earth. Man longs for peace apart from God! The apostle taught the cry of modern man prior to the judgment of God breaking upon his world would be the continual cry for peace and security. (I Thess. 5:3) Remember that he Anti-Christ according to Daniel 9:27 has made a peace covenant with Israel for seven year period. Anti-Christ is unable to bring peace to the earth. While Anti-Christ is ruling, God the Father is pouring out judgment upon the earth. Like the Iraqi crisis, all of this will come without any warning on our modern world.

The Third Seal Follows

The third seal, which is the black horse speaks of that which follows war, world-wide inflation and famine. (Rev. 6:5-6)

Seal Four

The fourth seal results in the logical consequence to war, inflation, and famine: death and Hell. "And I looked, and behold, an ashen horse; and he who sat on it had the name Death; and Hades was following with him." (Rev. 6:7-8) The astonishing impact of this judgment is that it kills two of the eight billion people then living on the earth. This is roughly the present population of North America, not one time but ten times. This incredible seal judgement of God kills two billion people from all over the earth.

Seal Five

The fifth seal reveals a religious holocaust that Israeli Christian saints and other tribulation saints will face for their faith in Christ. (Rev. 6:9) These tribulation saints beheaded at the beginning of the week, petition the Lord God for justice by avenging their killers. (Rev. 6:10) The request is given immediate attention by God the Father. (Rev. 6:11)

Earth Damaged

The sixth seal removes the permanence of creation by writing judgement on the earth and in the sky. Earthquake! The sun no longer gives its light! A darkness and a blackness is felt in the sky and over the face of the earth. Men in darkness is a figure of speech often to convey the spiritual blackness and the plight of men who have not trusted Christ as their personal Savior. John the Apostle develops the doctrine of the spiritual blindness and darkness of the world (kosmos) in his Gospel. Men apart from Christ live in a world of spiritual blindness. Their is a blindness over their eyes and spiritual sight to the person and life and work of Jesus Christ. Here, in the book of the Revelation, a figure of speech is used to convey literal meaning and truth. Yes, during the tribulation, the sun at this point will no longer give it's light. The moon becomes the color of blood. The stars of the sky fall to the earth! The sky is split. Mountains and islands split and move. Men long for death rather than face the God man Christ Jesus. The Scripture says: "and they said to the mountains and to the rocks, Fall on us and hide us from the presence of Him who sits on the throne, and from the wrath of the Lamb." (Rev. 6:16) Men want to be buried by the mountains and rocks which God has split (Rev. 6:14) rather than face the wrath of the Eternal Son of God Jesus Christ. Men longing for death rather than face the Wrath of the Eternal Son of God Jesus Christ. Men longing for death! Trust Christ Now! Escape the Coming Tribulation Wrath that will engulf our earth.

A Divine Pause

God pauses sealing and protecting the one-hundred and forty -four thousand Jewish evangelists. These are to proclaim the gospel to the Gentiles from the beginning of the final seven year period of man's history. This sealing of the 144,000 Jews has to do with the supernatural protecting hand of God sealing 12,000 from each of the 12 tribes. This direct supernatural of God is so that these 144,000 Jewish evangelists are able to fulfill their ministry. Revelation chapter 7 goes back to the very beginning of the week that seven year final period of God's judgment on the earth. (Rev. 7:1) Observe carefully the message of the angel of the Lord God in 7:2 and in Rev. 7:3: "Do not harm the earth or the sea or the trees, until we have sealed the bond-servants of our God on their foreheads." The 144,000 Jewish evangelists are sent throughout the earth the result of their ministry is the great redeemed multitude in Rev. 7:9-17. Once their ministry is completed the Lord God the Father by means of the Eternal Son of God breaks the seventh seal upon the earth.

Seal Judgment Seven

The seventh seal breaks forth into the seven trumpet judgments of God. "And when He broke the seventh seal, there was silence in heaven for about a half an hour." The Lord God gives the earth a half hour that is thirty minutes to repent. The seven trumpet judgments strike the earth from the midpoint of the seven year period until the end.

Man Makes No Response

Sad to say the earth makes no response to the Lord God! Earth does not repent would make a suitable newspaper heading on that day. The angels of God prepare themselves for the trumpet judgments. (Rev. 8:2)

The Seven Trumpet Judgments
Of God's Continued Wrath

These divine judgments are in rapid succession on the very environment of man. The first trumpet judgment burns up one third of all the trees on the earth. All the green grass is burned up on the earth. Hail and fire mixed with blood are cast down on the whole earth. (Rev. 8:7)

Trumpet two sounds! The seas are turned into blood. A third of all seas on the earth are turned into actual blood. A third of all sea life in the sea dies! One third of all ships were destroyed. (Rev. 8:8-9)

Trumpet three sounds! Man's water supply is struck by the Lord God! This judgment is on both rivers and springs. A third of all rivers and springs are contaminated on the earth by the Lord God. "Many men died from the waters, because they were made bitter." (Rev. 8:11)

Trumpet four sounds! This reduces the light on the earth by one third. The sun, moon and stars are all reduced by one third in their ability to radiate and reflect and luminate light. (Rev. 8:12)

Trumpet five sounds! Woe number one brings Demons who are kept in the pit loose on the earth to torment men.

Those without the seal of God on their foreheads are to be tormented for five months by the repeated stings of demons. The demons sting is like that of a scorpion. (Rev. 9:4-5) Note that by God's permission they are not allowed to kill anyone. (9:5) The Bible says that the first woe is now past and their are two woes still to come after their judgment falls on the earth. (Rev. 9:12)

Trumpet six sounds! The Red Chinese army is released upon the earth so that they might kill a third of men. (Rev. 9:15) We must remember earlier that it was in the first three and a half years of this seven year period, a quarter of the earth's population some two billion or two thousand million had been killed by one judgment of God. (Rev. 6:8) Yet man would not repent of his sin and start trusting Jesus as his Savior. Read Revelation 9:15-19 and think this very terrible judgment out! The Red Chinese are communists every bit as much as the Russians, red is red. Could China's nuclear pact treaties be a delay guarantee until she can maneuver her human wave army in the field? Yes, by Divine permission of heaven the Chinese and the oriental power block have their place and timing in the drama of the final three and a half years of the seven year period. The power and devastation of such an army is seen in Revelation 9:15 that they might kill a third of man.

The Red Chinese will murder two billion for God has decreed that this event will happen and the population involved is roughly ten times the present population of North America. This leaves about four to five billion people on the face of the earth.

How Can An Army Of
200 Million Kill 2000 Million Men?

The Bible teaches by portable nuclear weapons which soldiers can fire from their horses quite easily. (Rev. 9:18) Yet man does not repent, incredible! (Rev. 9:20-21)

Trumpet Seven

"And the seventh angel sounded; and there arose loud voices in heaven, saying: "The kingdom of this world has become the kingdom of our God and of His Christ; and He will reign forever and ever." (Rev. 11:15) Christ repossesses the earth by war. (see Rev. 11:15 but also Rev. 19:1-21)

The Seven Bowls of God's Wrath

The third series of God's direct judgments by supernatural intervention through the ministry of His good angels is found in Revelation 15 and 16. "And I saw another sign in heaven, great and marvelous, seven angels who had seven plagues, which are the last, because in them the wrath of God is finished." (Rev. 15:1)

Wrath of God

Mankind who worshiped the beast are afflicted with a cancerous sore. (Rev. 16:2) Bowl judgment two turns all seas and bodies of water into blood. Surely, men will be able to see the reflection by this graphic visual aid of necessity of approaching God on the basis of shed blood. The shed blood on the cross is the only sacrifice. Men must put personal trust in Christ's death to receive the forgiveness of sins. The third blast of God's wrath is on all rivers and springs of water which are turned into blood. (Rev. 16: 4) This judgment is with good reason as we look at Revelation 16:5-17 because of the earth pouring out the blood of the Christians by martyring them to death. The fourth bowl is on men who are scorched with fire from the sun. (Rev. 16:8) Judgment five is a direct land strike on the throne of the world dictator and the false prophet. The removal of their authority is a judgment from heaven over the earth. (Rev. 16:10) The sixth bowl gathers the armies of the earth to the Battle of Armageddon. (Rev. 16:12-16) The oriental power block is a judgment of God upon the earth. Three demons deceive the remaining power blocks on the earth probably with the promise of world power. (Rev. 16:14-16)

"And they gathered them together to the place which in Hebrew is called Harmagedon." (Rev. 16:16)

The final bowl judgment finishes the judgement program of God upon the earth. (Rev. 16:17) A great earthquake wrings the earth with the greatest devastation of any earth quake in the history of man. Rome is split into three parts by this terrible judgment of God. Every city of the Gentiles fell. (Rev. 16:19) Islands move! "The mountains were not found." (Rev. 16:20) Men are further struck and killed by one hundred pound hailstones. (Rev. 16:21) Does man repent? Man will not repent even after all these judgments of God. Men responded wrongly instead of repenting of their sin they cursed God. (Rev. 16:21) The Lord God of heaven has judged His earth!

• • • • •

Chapter Two Study Questions

1. What did John the Apostle see as recorded in the book of Revelation chapters 4 and 5?

2. How is Revelation chapter 6 to be understood?

3. Who are the 144,000 in Revelation chapter 7?

4. What are the trumpet judgments of Revelation chapter 8?

5. What purpose do the bowl judgments of the book of Revelation chapter 15 serve?

Challenge Questions

1. What is God's purpose for Red China in the Armageddon calendar?

2. How can a tribulation sinner escape the wrath of the Eternal Son of God Jesus Christ?

3
Nuclear Weapons In The End Times

The Middle East Is Arming

Jew and Arab arm themselves with nuclear weapons and continue to arm themselves. Arab will power desires a bomb comparable to the one that Israel is known to possess.

Zechariah Predicted The Coming Nuclear Holocaust!

Zechariah teaches with one hundred percent accuracy the answers to the questions relating to Israel, the Arab world, nuclear war, the problem facing Israel of hostile neighbors, the problem of disarmament, the winds of Anti-Jewish sentiment and the all out nuclear holocaust which is to follow. Yes, Zechariah the Bible prophet along with the prophet Haggai came from Persia (modern Iran) to encourage the remnant who returned to build the temple in Jerusalem. His ministry historically was from 520 to 485 B.C. while Israel was coming out of the Babylonian Medio-Persia captivity.

The Context of Zechariah 8 to 11

The Lord God had disciplined the nation by giving the northern kingdom in 722 B.C. to the Assyrians. The Southern kingdom of Judah and Benjamin had been given into the hands of the Babylonians in 586 B.C.

Jerusalem had been sacked and destroyed by the conquering Babylonians. The question in the mind of the Jew was: What is the plan of God for Jerusalem?

God Will Do Good To Jerusalem

"For thus says the Lord of hosts, 'Just as I purposed to do harm to you when your fathers provoked Me to wrath,' says the Lord of hosts, 'and I have not relented, so I have again purposed in these days to do good to Jerusalem and to the house of Judah: "Do not fear!" (Zechariah 8:14-15)

Zechariah 8 deals with the blessings of the Lord God on Judah and Jerusalem in the end times. However, the Bible presents to us the problem that Israel faces her hostile neighbors in chapter 9.

Israel's Enemies Predicted in Zechariah 9

Syria, Lebanon and Jordan in the end times are predicted as three of Israel's hostile and angry neighbors. How is that for accuracy? The blessings of God upon Judah and Jerusalem cannot be realized unless these angry and hostile neighbors are defeated. Messiah Jesus Christ is the One to defeat and disarm those hostile Arab neighbors. "And I will cut off the chariot from Ephraim, and the horse from Jerusalem; and the bow will be cut off. And He (Jesus Christ) will speak peace to the nations." (Zechariah 9:10) It is within the same context that the New Testament writers pick the verse out where Christ is predicted by Zechariah to ride upon the donkey presenting Himself to the nation Israel as Messiah in 33 A.D.

While Syria is mentioned specifically in Zechariah 9 as the prime enemy of Israel, Lebanon and Jordan are as well additional enemies in Zechariah 11:1-3. They want to prevent the fulfillment of Israel's hope and blessings.

What Is Israel's Real Problem?

Zechariah teaches that the nation in the end times is under false leadership in addition to the Arab threat. The present leaders of Israel are depicted in the Word of God as false shepherds in Zechariah 10:1-3. The Scripture says: "They (Israel) are afflicted because there is no shepherd." (Zechariah 10:2d) The Lord God will cleanse the nation of these false shepherds. "My anger is kindled against the shepherds, And I will punish the male goats (leaders); For the Lord of hosts has visited His flock, the house of Judah, and will make them like His majestic horse in battle." (Zechariah 10:3)

A National Regathering of Israel- Zechariah 10:4-11:3

The unwise leadership of the present day in Israel will bring Israel into a death struggle with her hostile neighbors and the Gentile nations of the world. (Zechariah 10:4-7) Israel will be saved by the true Messiah and the rightful leader in Israel Jesus the Christ. (Zechariah 10:4-7) Following the battle and dispersion of Judah, Messiah Jesus Christ will regather the Jews from the entire earth to Israel. Why? They will face judgment before their Messiah Jesus Christ and their right or the lack of it to enter into the millennial kingdom. (Zechariah 10:8-12)

Jesus Rejected- The First Time Round

In Zechariah chapter 11, we see the terrible mistake that Israel made prophesied by Zechariah during the 6th century B.C. fulfilled during the time of Christ on the earth 30-33 A.D. The rejection of Jesus by the nation, is found in (Zechariah 11:7-14). Zechariah role plays the true Messiah in His Rejection. Messiah fed the flock. (Zechariah 11:7) Dr. Charles Feinberg says: "We are not left long in doubt as to the results of the shepherd ministry now before us. In one month, in a comparatively short time, the shepherd found it necessary to cut off the

32

three shepherds over the nation. The soul of the shepherd wearied of them and their soul hated him." (C.L. Feinberg, The Minor Prophets, p. 327.) Zechariah depicting Messiah breaks His staff Beauty. (Zechariah 11:10) "Zechariah is speaking of the nations of the earth, and he reveals an important truth-God has made a covenant with the peoples of the earth relative to His own people Israel. He has placed them under restraint lest they work Israel harm or ill....When the restraint was removed, the Romans destroyed their city and economy." (Feinberg, Minor Prophets, p. 328) The destruction took place in 70 A.D. by Titus and the Romans.

Now Messiah depicted by Zechariah asks the nation Israel for their gratitude for His ministry. Instead, the nation Israel insulted Messiah by paying him the price of a worthless slave! (Zechariah 11:12) According to Exodus 21:32, this is the price of a gored slave! Zechariah 11:13 is quoted by Matthew as fulfilled by the Lord Jesus' betrayal by Judas in Mt. 27:10 and the results of this wicked deed. The breaking of the second staff by Zechariah predicted the dissolution of the brotherhood between Judah and Israel. "This was surely fulfilled in the sad scene during the siege of Jerusalem by the Romans under Titus. There was a breaking up of the social fabric of the Jewish nation. Internal strife and divisions were prevalent and contributed largely to the downfall of Judea." (Feinberg, p. 329)

The False Shepherd

Israel will accept the wicked shepherd the Anti-Christ during the Tribulation period. (Zechariah 11:15-17)

The Middle East Blows

Zechariah 12-14 presents all the Gentile nations of the earth gathered against Israel to force Israel to submit to their authority. (Zechariah 12:2-6) Jerusalem will be three things to the nations that come against her (1) a cup of wrath-the nations will stagger like a drunkard (2) a millstone-so that all those who fool with Jerusalem will be ground to pieces. (3) A Firepot and a torch suggesting destruction of the nations.

Jesus the Christ the true Messiah the Bible teaches will defend Judah and Jerusalem. Jesus will fight for Israel. (Zechariah 12:8) All the nations of the earth will be gathered against Judah and Jerusalem. The Lord Jesus will destroy these nations that come against Israel. (Zechariah 12:3 & 9)

The Nation Israel Repents

The national mourning (repentance) by Israel will be followed by the acceptance of Jesus Christ as their Messiah. (Zechariah 12:10-14) The national conversion of the nation will take place at the Second Advent of Christ.

First Israel Defeated

Zechariah 14 presents the nation Israel in a picture of defeat and emotional shock.

Then Messiah Redeems Them

Zechariah 12 to 14 presents Israel in a helpless and defenseless position. Jerusalem is captured! "The houses plundered, the women ravished, and half of the city exiled, but the rest of the people will not be cut off from the city." (Zechariah 14:2) Israel is purged by these invasions in which two-thirds of the nation perishes and one third is awaiting Messiah. (Zechariah 13:8-9) These chapters deal with one theme Gentile nations gathered together against Jerusalem. In these chapters, one of the battles of close fighting in the streets of Jerusalem within the campaign battles of Armageddon is presented to us.

The nation had it not been for Messiah Jesus Christ whom they had rejected and crucified would have been wiped out! Christ gets the attention of the Nation and the nations of the world by splitting the Mount of Olives. (Zechariah 14:4) He (Jesus Christ) provides a valley through which the persecuted Israel can flee to safety to the other side of the City. (Zechariah 14:5)

Nations Struck With Plague

The Lord Jesus strikes the nations with a divine plague. (Zechariah 14:12) A great tumult breaks out and results in panic and confusion, the Gentile soldiers begin to kill each other. (Zechariah 14:13) This divine plague spreads to all life even the animal world. (Zechariah 14:15)

When Did Christ Return?

The word "then" in Zechariah 14:3 points to the continuing sequence of events. Jesus Christ returns to fight for Israel at the end of the seven year tribulation period. Zechariah 14:3 pictures the Lord Jesus going forth to war against the nations of the earth. The nations are conquered! The Day of The Lord is that period of wrath on the earth when the Lord God deals with Israel and the nations of the earth in Judgment and retribution.

Nuclear War

Jesus spoke on "How History Will End?" He indicated a time of catastrophe to be dealt to the world, which unless the God head stepped in to shorten, the history of the race would end in total annihilation. The threat to the entire civilization on such a scale must be nuclear war. Yes, Matthew 24:22 does not say nuclear war, yet such is implied from the words of Jesus.

Bible Teaches Nuclear Weapons Will Be Used

Zechariah 14:12 is a clear reference to the use of nuclear weapons during the final world conflict. "Now this will be the plague with which the Lord will strike all the peoples who go to war against Jerusalem: their flesh will rot while they stand on their feet, and their eyes will rot in their sockets, and their tongues will rot in their mouth." This is a clear reference to the use of nuclear weapons and warfare during the final world conflict.

The Chinese Use Nuclear Weapons Effectively

The major use of nuclear weapons is wielded effectively by the Chinese as taught in the book of Revelation 9:13-19. The Russians are not to be feared as much as the Chinese as they are used in the Sovereign Judgment of God against the earth. Yes, the Chinese are predestined in the eternal plan of God the Father, the Eternal Son Jesus Christ and the Holy Spirit to use nuclear weapons to kill one-third of the three-quarters of the earth's population left during the Tribulation period. This destructive and devastating blow to the human race results in approximately 916 thousand million deaths. "A third of mankind was killed by these three plagues, by the fire and the smoke and the brimstone, which proceeded out of their mouths." (Rev. 9:18) Read the Armageddon chapter!

Chapter Three Study Questions

1. What picture does Zechariah 12 to 14 paint?

2. Who saves Israel?

3. What is Israel saved from?

4. Will nuclear weapons be used in the final world conflict?

5. What purpose do the Chinese serve during this time?

Challenge Questions

1. How is Matthew 24:22 to be interpreted?

2. How is Zechariah 14:12 to be interpreted?

• • • • •

4
Armageddon

Three Russian Armies

The Bible teaches the great military might and strength of Russia "in the end times." The Russian bear is able to equip and maneuver three complete armies in the field. The King of the North plays it's part in the 70th week of Daniel the final 7 year period of history for the world and the nation of Israel. The truth of the three Russian armies fighting in the Armageddon campaign is found in Ezekiel 38 and 39, Daniel 11:40-43 and Daniel 11:44.

When Russia Begins To March

Some Bible expositors have thought that Russia attacks Israel at the beginning of the period known as the Tribulation. Others have held that Russia attacks Israel at the middle of the week of the 7 year period. (3 1/2 year point) A further opinion is that Israel is attacked at the end of the seven year period in the final battle of the Armageddon campaign. The question of Russian aggression is seen clearly in Ezekiel 38 and 39. The picture presented to us is one of Russia fulfilling the divine decree of God when Israel is living without any need of self protection. Russia attacks Israel (Ezekiel 38:10-11). The land described as needing no protection is the land of Israel. (Ezekiel 38:16 and 38:18)

The invasion of Israel by Russia must be close to the middle of the 7 year period because Anti-Christ persecutes Israel during the last half of the seven year period. Prior to this attack on the Jews, Israel is seen living securely in their own land protected by Anti-Christ. The picture presented to us in the prophecy of Ezekiel 38:11 is Israel "the land of unwalled villages." The first three and a half years is the period of peace for Israel, the false Christ and the world church.

Will Russia Rule The World?

Russia will continue to be a world power but will never be a World Empire. This deduction is a conclusion based on Daniel chapters 2 and 7. Babylon (Iraq), Medio-Persia, Greece, Rome and the yet to be revised Roman Empire and finally Christ's millennial kingdom are the six world empires outlined and decreed by God in the Bible. Babylon, Medio-Persia, Greece, and Rome have run their courses and are a part of the past historical period. The Revised Roman Empire and Christ's Millennial Kingdom are future World Empires and will yet come upon the earth. Communism is being used by God to prepare the world for judgment in the form of the worship of a man Anti-Christ. Communism and the Russians will not conquer and rule the entire world. The answer is simple enough because God the Father has not decreed it in Eternity Past and the Bible does not predict the triumph but rather the fall of the Russians.

Russia Attacks

Russia is clearly referred to in Ezekiel chapter 38 and 39 as Gog, Rosh, Meschech and Tubal. Russia is identified clearly for us in Ezekiel as "coming from your place out of the remote parts of the north." The remotest and farthest point due north from Israel is Russia. (Ezekiel 38:15 & 39:2)

Russia is clearly identified as the nation to attack

Israel in Desert Storm II from the grammar in the text. Gog is a person or leader of the land of Magog. Ma is a prefix for place in Coptic. Rosh contains the consonants of Russia. Gog is the prince of Rosh. The grammatical changes in the word Meschech can be traced to Moschoi and ultimately Moscow. Tubal is easily identified with one of the modern provinces of Russia.

Russia's Allies

Who attacks Israel with Russia? Arab and African nations join Russia to share so they think in Israel's wealth. (Ezekiel 38:11 & 12) Egypt, Put, Lud, all Arabia, Libya and the people of the land are all seen to come against Israel in Ezekiel 30:4. This time of doom for the nations is part of the events of the Old Testament period of judgment yet with a future fulfillment taking place prior to the Second Advent of Christ. Ethiopia which is referred to as the nation Cush in Scripture is even in our present day a place of suffering and death due to Russian activity and propaganda. Red Communism presenting itself as a Savior to the African world.

Put is easily identified as modern day Libya. (Ezekiel 30:5, 38:5) Lud is a representative of the African nations. "All Arabia" supports Egypt. (Ezekiel 30:5) Even the "P.L.O." is specifically predicted: "the people of the land that is in league will fall with them." (Ezekiel 30:5) Remember, Ezekiel is in Babylon receiving this revelation and writing the prophetic truth in the 6th century B.C. Persia is the nation of Iran. Iran is a Russian ally when they attack Israel. (Ezekiel 38:5) Germany is reunited and sides with Russia. The Bible predicts Gomer with all its troops. The Talmud identifies Gomer as Germany. Beth-Togarmah is Armenia or modern day Turkey long known to be communist. (Ezekiel 38:6)

Desert Storm II

The Russian confederacy and her allies receives only a verbal rebuke from the Western world. Sheba, Dedan, the merchants of Tarshish and the young lions are to be identified as follows in terms of modern nations in our present day scenario. Sheba and Dedan are identified as certain Arab peoples. Tarshish is identified with Great Britain and the young lions as the British commonwealth colonies and the United States of America.

Israel Will Be Attacked

"And you (Russia) will go up, you will come like a STORM; you will be like a cloud covering the land, you and all your troops, and many peoples with you." (Ezekiel 38:9) Ezekiel continues to say: "And you come up against my people Israel like a cloud to cover the land." (Ezekiel 38:16)

Communist World Judged

Russian troops and her allies cover the land like a STORM. (Ezekiel 38:9) To capture the wealth of the Middle East! (Ezekiel 38:12) Riding on horses! (Ezekiel 38:4) The Lord God supernaturally intervenes and destroys them. (Ezekiel 38:19) The Lord God creates chaos and confusion. An epidemic breaks out! Fire and brimstone fall from heaven. (Ezekiel 38:22-23) Three Hundred and Sixty Million people converge on the land of Israel. This is a considerable contrast to the total man power of W.W. II which was 42 million. The number 360 million was arrived at based on the text of Ezekiel where it will take 7 months to bury the dead. (Ezekiel 39:11-12)

Marxist-Lenin Doctrine Judged By God

The Lord God reverses the atheistic preaching of their communist doctrine by proclaiming Himself to the nations and to Israel in their unbelief. Earlier, Israel had accepted the Anti-Christ and made a peace treaty with him. (Daniel 9:27) "And I shall set My glory among the nations; and all the nations will see My judgement which I have executed, and My hand which I have laid on them. And the house of Israel will know that I am the Lord their God-from that day onward." (Ezekiel 39:21-22)

A Divine Lesson

The Gentile nations of the earth will understand the reason for Israel's sufferings and her hardships through the centuries. (Ezekiel 39:23-24)

World Dictator declares himself to be God in the Middle East! The balance of power has changed in the world with the destruction of the first Russian army and her allies. (Daniel 11:36-39)

Dictator Declares War

This Anti-Christ known as the beast in Scripture moves his headquarters to the Beautiful Land. (Daniel 11:41) Israel, the land of Palestine is characterized for its beauty in the Bible. In line with the dictatorship of the world dictator the Bible declares: "and many countries will fall;....Then he will stretch out his hand against other countries, and the land of Egypt will not escape." (Daniel 11:41-42) Anti-Christ conquers and controls Egypt at this mid-point of the final 7 year period of human history. The Libyans and the Ethiopians launch a counter offensive against the western leader. (Daniel 11:43) At this time, the great military might of Russia is revealed as the Red Communists are able to launch a second army, an attack against the Anti-Christ. (Daniel 11:40)

Desert Storm II Battle Two

Egypt and Russia attack the Dictator, Daniel predicts! (Daniel 11:40)

Sleeping Dragon Awakes

The Red Chinese and the other Oriental powers enter the picture at this point in the death struggle for world power, rule and dominion. The human wave enters the Holy Land with a man power of 200 hundred million men approximately five times the total man power of World War II. (Rev. 9:16). (See also Rev. 16:12-16)

The Place In Hebrew Called Har-Magedon

The three demons are used by the dragon (Satan) and the beast (world dictator) and the false prophet to gather all the nations of the earth to the Battle of Armageddon. (Rev. 16:16)

Sign Of The Son Of Man

The Sign of the Son of Man has appeared in the sky for some 45 days. (Matthew 24:30) The Lord Jesus, Israel's true Messiah comes from heaven with heaven's armies to destroy the beast, the King of the North (Russia), and the oriental horde. (Revelation 19:11-16) The beast (world dictator) and the Kings of the Earth and their armies make war against Christ. (Revelation 19:19)

Son of Man Destroys His Enemies

The beast and the false prophet are thrown into the lake of fire which burns with fire and brimstone and in which they will be tormented forever and ever. (Revelation 19:20)
"And the rest were killed with the sword which came from the mouth of him (Jesus Christ) who sat upon the horse, and all the birds were filled with their flesh." (Rev. 19:21)

Chapter Four Study Questions

1. What does Daniel 11:40-43 teach us about Russia?

2. What does Daniel 11:44 tell us about the Russian nation?

3. What insight does Ezekiel 38 and 39 give us?

4. Will Russia rule the world?

5. Who are Russia's allies in the end times?

Challenge Questions

1. What opposition does the free world offer to the attack described in Ezekiel 38 and 39?

2. What does the prophet tell us about Desert Storm II?

• • • • •

5
Three Questions

Many questions have been asked through the ages about Jerusalem and the shaping of events in the Middle East. The Jewish people responded in Matthew 27:25 referring to Jesus Christ: "His blood be upon us and our children." (Mt. 27:25) Twenty centuries have come and gone with this statement looming largely over the Jewish people. Has Israel deserved the suffering that has befallen them because of their rejection of Jesus as their Messiah?

Jesus pronounced judgment upon all that constituted the life of the nation in 33 A.D. (1) Israel's leaders Mt. 23:13 (2) Jerusalem Mt. 23:37-39 (3) The Temple Proper Mt. 24:1-2 This partial judgment fell on the nation when Titus and the Romans destroyed Israel in 70 A.D.

Jesus was asked three questions by his disciples which are the basis for His presentation of the truth to His disciples. The disciples began to question the Lord on the theme of how "Jewish age" will end? Put in contemporary language of the present scenario "how is the conflict in the Middle East going to end?" (Mt. 24:3)

Question 1 When will these things be?

Question 2 What will be the sign of your coming?

Question 3 What will be the sign of the end?

Three Answers

Question 3 was answered first by Christ as He sat upon the Mount of Olives. What will be the Sign of the End? Now Jesus being God knew the minds of the disciples that they understood that 7 years were left upon God's prophetic time clock once that clock began to tick. Jesus summarized for us the signs (indicators-events) of the first 3 1/2 years in Matthew 24:3-8.

Sign 1   Religious Deception (Mt. 24:4)
Sign 2   False Messiahs and Prophets (Mt. 24:5)
Sign 3   News of Wars and Rumors of Wars (Mt. 24:6)
Sign 4   Civil Wars (Mt. 24:7)
Sign 5   International Unrest (Mt. 24:7)
Sign 6   Famine (Mt. 24:7)
Sign 7   Earthquakes (Mt. 24:7)

Jesus compared all these signposts in Mt. 24:4-7 to a woman who is experiencing labor pains and about to give birth to a baby. The labor pains intensify and become more severe contractions as delivery time approaches. While these signs are true of any age, they intensify as our world enters into the tribulation period.

Signs of the 2nd half of the 7 year period begin while the signs of the first 3 1/2 years continue throughout the last half of the 7 year period.

[Seven Years of Time Left on God's Prophetic Clock]
[3 1/2   ][3 1/2]
    Matthew 24:3-8   Matthew 24:9-14
                            Mt. 24:3-8
                            Continues

Signs 8 to 14 Begin Matthew 24:9-14

Sign 8   Betrayal and Tribulation (Mt. 24:9-10)
Sign 9   Great Religious Deception (Mt.24:11)
Sign 10 Lawlessness Increases (Mt. 24:12)
Sign 11 Jewish Christians Must Endure (Mt. 24:13)
Sign 12 The King Is Coming (Mt. 24:14)

Sign 13   Major Sign of the Last 3 1/2 years of the 7 year period is the proclamation of Anti-Christ as God and his demand to be worshiped as God. (Mt. 24:15)

Sign 14   The Persecution of Israel   (Mt. 24:16-20)

The right response to Persecution is to flee! Travel is difficult and especially hard for those with child and new mothers. Jesus tells the tribulation Jewish saints of that future day to pray that their persecution will not come in the winter for it will be cold and not on the Sabbath. They might be trapped when AntiChrist who is there in the Jewish place of worship persecutes.

Sign 15   Human Race Comes To Brink of Destruction (Mt. 24:22)

The human race would destroy itself without divine intervention by the Father and His Son Jesus. The ability of man realized through nuclear weapons is stopped by God so that the race will not annihilate itself. For the sake of the elect those tribulation saints who trust Christ as their Messiah and Savior, God the Father will step in sooner than the previously planned time so that the tribulation saints who are alive may be spared. Although many tribulation saints have been martyred see Revelation 7:9-17 and 16:3-7.

Sign 16   The Ministry of the Second Beast - The False Prophet (Mt. 24:23).

"For false christs and false prophets will arise and give great signs and wonders, so that to deceive (with this result), if possible (1st class condition assumes the reality of the fact--it will be true and come about) also the elect." (Greek New Testament)

The sixteen signs given by Christ upon the Mount of Olives predict the end of Middle East history. This was in response to the question asked by the disciples: "What will be the Sign of the End?"

Question 2 is answered next by Jesus as to the Sign of His Coming. This question relates to the time immediately after the Tribulation period of 7 years. The background painted by Christ is a black darkness over the earth, and a blackness that men in that day will feel.

"But immediately after the tribulation of those days the sun will be darkened, and the moon will not give its light and the stars will fall from the heaven, and the powers of Heavens will be shaken." (Mt. 24:29 Greek New Testament)

After The Tribulation

Sign 1 The Son of Man

"And then the Sign of the Son of Man will appear in heaven." (Mt. 24:30) The sign of the Son of Man the shekinah glory of God will illuminate the darkness of the sky. Mt.24:30 It is the second Coming of Jesus Christ to rule with authority and great power the nations of the earth.

"And then all the tribes of the earth will mourn, and they will see the son of man coming on the clouds of the heaven with power and great glory." (Mt. 24:30)

Sign 2 Israel Regathered

Israel is regathered from their dispersion throughout the world to face Messiah Jesus Christ in judgment.

"And he will send forth his angels with a great trumpet and they will gather together his elect from the four winds, from one end of the heavens to the other." (Mt. 24:31)

Every Jew will be brought back to the Holy Land to face Messiah in judgment. Judgment precedes entrance into the kingdom. (Mt. 24:40-41)

"One shall be taken [in judgment] and one shall enter [into the kingdom.]"

The kingdom is Christ's millennial rule of 1000 years'

48

reign on the earth. (David's kingdom)

Question 1 is answered last by Jesus as to: "When will these things be?"

"Now learn the parable from the fig tree." (Mt. 24:32)

As the fig tree's branches sent forth sprouts and foliage appeared, so one knew the approach of summer: "so you too when you see all these things, know that it is near, right at the door." (Mt. 24:33) One would know the certainty of the end as he saw all these signs unfolding before his eyes.

Sign 3 Judgement on Living Israel

Living Israel will face judgment as taught by the parable of the good and wise virgins and those who were unwise. (Mt. 25:1-13)

Sign 4 Judgment on the Gentiles

The Nations will be judged by the Lord Jesus at the end of tribulation prior to the millennial kingdom on their treatment of the Jew during the tribulation. This truth is taught in the sheep and goat judgment in Matthew 25:31-46. The Jew is persecuted during the tribulation without food or shelter. The Gentiles who were saved during the tribulation demonstrate their faith in Christ by their works, (Mt. 25:37-40). The righteous Gentiles will be taken into the millennial kingdom, (Mt. 25:34). The unrighteous Gentiles will be put in Hell because they did not demonstrate their genuine faith in the Messiah Jesus Christ by their works. (Mt. 25:41-46)

Growing Anxiety And Phobia

Yes, the Middle East is a powder keg with current tensions simmering between Arab world and the Jewish factions now united because of the Iraqi war, and Heaven's use of this mad dictator to God's Glory. What is the real scoop on Israel?

Chapter Five Study Questions

1. What 3 questions did the disciples ask Jesus?

2. What answers did Christ give to those questions?

3. What are signs 1 to 7 in the end times?

4. What are signs 8 to 14 in the end times?

5. What is the major sign of the time of Jacob's trouble?

Challenge Questions

1. What 5 prophetic events are yet future according to Matthew 24 and 25?

2. What three practical responses does Matthew give in the light of these 5 prophetic events?

6
What Are The Israeli's Thinking?

What will happen to the nation of Israel? Does Israel as a people and a nation have a national hope? If Israel gave up her land in the Middle East wouldn't it bring about an everlasting peace in the Middle East and the rest of the world? The Flame organization in the U.S. News & World Report gives the Arab Moslem as the real cause for unrest in the Middle East. The Arab Moslem states desire to destroy Israel and their hatred and intolerance is fueled, pardon the pun, by Arab Moslem fanaticism.

Today, the Jewish position some suggest has become a commitment to the hardliners of yesteryear. The hardline position having a historical precedent only once in the history of the nation Israel. Masada! Is the Israeli position harder today than during the Menachem Begin era? At one time the Israeli's thought their problems solvable through their own resources.

New Israeli Rhetoric

The New Israeli rhetoric is the statement of belief that only force can solve the present peril to Israel's existence by Arab power and the Western world. A new argument is being beamed out of Israel today. Israel is moving in an entirely new direction predicted by the prophets as one of the excesses to avoid. Zechariah presents the picture of false shepherds "current leaders" who bring the nation into a death struggle. Religious nationalism calling for Israeli alert to survival in a hostile world forever is heralded forth by rhetoricians.

51

A Dark Force

The Israeli's perceive a dark force at work in the modern Zionist state dividing them into two camps. The hardliners are preaching an emotional message romanticizing the glory of war, victory and "the greatest good" to offer one's life for his country. Some have interpreted this position as an excess which excesses were warned against by the prophets. This religious romanticism finds her glory in isolation from the world. Will a fortress Israel only speed up their final chapter of history?

Shamir thought the creation of a Palestinian state a threat to the very existence of his nation. (U.S. News & World Report - 4/16/90)

No Recognition, No Negotiation, No Peace With Israel

The Arab position has not changed from the Israeli victory in 1967. The Arab doctrine expounded that followed was no recognition of Israel, no negotiation with Israel, and no peace with Israel. Israel's interpretation of succession to Arabs of Judea, Samaria (the West Bank) and Gaza region can only become Arab inroads for the total destruction of Israel. The real conflict is with the Arab nations not just the Palestinians. All Arabia with the exception of Egypt are avowed to a continuous state of no recognition, no negotiation, and no peace with Israel.

The Israeli's will not give up their land without a fight that battle in the Scripture is called Armageddon. Nuclear war and destruction follow and all of mankind would be wiped out.

Red Russian Communist Aggression

The Russian bid for domination in the Middle East is indirect because of the oil rich Middle East fields and the wealth of the area. The Russian bear if in control of the Middle East will be able to control Western Europe who have been dependent upon imported oil from the Middle East.

The God Of Heaven

The God of Heaven declares eternal blessing or curse upon the nations of the world in relationship to their treatment of the Jew. The Sovereign God of Heaven is moving all of history to enthrone Jesus Christ upon a millennial throne from Jerusalem.

Is The "World" Stumbling To Armageddon?

The strategy is clear a hard line Israeli position! No concession! Arab determination to wipe out Israel. The Arabs hold the key bargaining point the oil. The West and the world turn against Israel to solve their own dilemma for survival. Isolated Israel will not give up her land. Armageddon ensues!

The Battle Against Israel

The Bible declares that the God of heaven gathers the nations to do battle against Israel. Zephaniah, Zechariah and Joel confirm the movement of heaven upon the Gentile powers and their alliances. Yes, the Lord God of Heaven is going to gather all the nations of the earth together against Israel. (Zech. Chapters 12 to 14)

What Is Israel's Hope?

Israel keeps hanging on because of the covenants that the Lord God made with their fathers, the patriarchs. These covenants are the Abrahamic, Palestinian, the Davidic and the New Covenant heralded by Jeremiah the prophet.

The Abrahamic Covenant promises the Middle East to Israel. The Middle East is Israel's land. The Covenant that the Lord God made with Abraham promises and guarantees that Israel will continue as a nation and a people forever. (Genesis 12, 15 & 17)

The Palestinian covenant promised Israel the repossession of her land. (Deuteronomy 30)

The Davidic Covenant promises Jesus Christ will deliver Israel at His Second Coming and will rule on David's Throne forever. (2 Samuel 7)

The New Covenant promises Israel trusts Jesus Christ at His Second Advent. (Jeremiah 31:31-37)

The biblical covenants guarantee the future right of the nation Israel both to their permanence as a nation and the possession of the Middle East land. What philosophical questions does this kind of promise raise for the Gentile nations? A lot of "What if" questions follow given Jewish belief in the covenants at least by the more Orthodox Jew; although the nation is for the large part back in the Holy Land at present in unbelief after the many traumatic centuries of the Jewish saga.

A more detailed exposition of each of the Covenants can be obtained from the author.

When Israel Will Not Give Up Her Land?

The Jew believes that the issue is not give up your land or parts of it so that peace will eventuate with the Arab. The real issue is the Arab's desire to bring about the complete destruction and annihilation of the Jewish state and people.

Some more orthodox Jews believe that the land is theirs because the Lord God gave the Middle East to Abraham and his seed forever. The Abrahamic covenant is an eternal and unconditional covenant.

A State of Unbelief

Israel is back in the land in a state of unbelief. The prophet Ezekiel pictures for us a revival of Israel and their national hope. In Ezekiel 37, the prophet is given a vision of Israel in a lifeless spiritual condition. The allegory is interpreted for us in 37:11: "Then He said to me, Son of Man, these bones are the whole house of Israel; behold, they say, our bones are dried up, and our hope has perished. They (house of Israel) have been cut off to us." Ezekiel 37:11 & 12 speak of the national hope of being regathered as a nation into their land. The national conversion of the nation is a wonderful truth to be found in 37:12-14. In all of this, the prophet Ezekiel is not referring to the physical resurrection of the dead but the spiritual revival and national conversion of the nation as a complete nation to trust Jesus Christ.

Is Their Hope Not Fulfilled Today?

Isn't the fact that the Jew is back in the land today a fulfillment of the "times of the Gentiles?" The times of the Gentiles is a period of rule that began with the fall of the city of Jerusalem in 586 B.C. at the hands of Nebuchadnezzar a former Iraqi king and the Gentiles will continue to rule until the Second Coming of Christ. Luke 21:20-24 is a tribulation context which will not be fulfilled until the time that Gentile armies of the nations of the world surround Jerusalem. The fullness of the Gentiles referred to in Romans 11:25 is the day of Gentile blessing to hear the gospel and be saved. Israel, by way of contrast, is set aside in unbelief.

Chapter Six Study Questions

1. What is the new Israeli rhetoric?

2. What dark force do some Israeli's see at work hanging over the nation?

3. What is the Arab doctrine toward Israel since 1967?

4. Why would Russia want control of the Middle East oil fields?

5. What do the Jewish covenants guarantee Israel?

Challenge Questions

1. What is the present spiritual *state of Israel?*

2. When will the times of the Gentiles be fulfilled?

• • • • •

Iraq

What does the Bible say about Iraq?

7
Are The Iraqi's To Be Found In The Bible?

This is an entirely different question from the one that people are asking is the Iraqi aggression of Kuwait to be found in the Bible? Is Iraq referred to as rebuilding in the prophets and the Book of Revelation? It is my purpose to answer each of these questions because an answer is to be found in each individual case. Is Iraq referred to in the prophets and the book of Revelation as rebuilding their kingdom in these end times? (Signs of The End Times) The Bible refers clearly to Iraq in both Isaiah and Jeremiah that Babylon the biblical nation will never be rebuilt. Dr. Chafer the founder and first President of Dallas Theological Seminary in Volume VII on pages 29-30: "Of the theory that the ancient city will yet be rebuilt for it to be destroyed in fulfillment of prediction, little can be said in its favor." (L.S. Chafer, Systematic Theology, Vol. VII, pp. 29-30.) The prophet Isaiah in Isaiah 13:19-22 and the prophet Jeremiah in Jeremiah 51:61-64 very clearly stated that Babylon the city would never be rebuilt. The Glory that was Nebuchadnezzar's in Babylon was never to be rebuilt with any lasting duration or significance in Biblical prophecy. The Bible does not predict the rebuilding of Iraq as a fulfillment of Biblical prophecy made by the prophets. The other error in the science of biblical interpretation (hermeneutics) is to interpret the Book of Revelation chapter 18, Babylon as modern day Iraq rather than the city of Rome. The Apostle Peter refers to Rome the city as Babylon at the end of his first epistle.

The aggression of Iraq against Kuwait and the unrest in the Middle East with Saddam Hussein is not mentioned in the Bible according to Dr. John F. Walvoord. (Kindred Spirit, Winter-Spring issue, 1991). The Bible does not speak of the Iraqi aggression of Kuwait in the Middle East.

What does the Bible say about Iraq? Iraq can be traced in the Table of Nations in Genesis chapter 10 to be a descendant of Noah's son Ham. (Genesis 10:6-10) The old biblical nation of Babylon but not the city itself is the forerunner of modern day Iraq. The location of modern day Iraq is the very location of the old biblical nation of Babylon. When man builds in defiance of what God's word decrees, is it any wonder that their monuments to self lie in ruins? Genesis 10:10 tells us of the beginning of the nation Babylon in Bible times began with Nimrod who was a son of Cush who was a son of Ham. Ham was one of the three sons of Noah who helped repopulate the earth after the biblical universal flood. Iraq is a revival of the old nation of Babylon which lived on the plain of Shinar.

Babylon now Iraq was divided then into a Northern and a Southern Kingdom. The north contained the cities of Accad and Babel. Southern Babylon was called Sumer and Erech was prominent city within Sumer.

The Bible traces the origin of the Iraq nation not to the Arab world but to the Gentile world who are descendants of Noah's son Ham. Yes, I have already said this but the point of importance is that the Iraqi's are not Arabs but Gentiles. This may well account for their close kinship with the Palestinians, and with their leader. The Jew remember traces his ancestry to Abraham. The Iraqi is thought to be Arab simply because of his proximity to the Middle East and tanned skin. The Arabs are descendants of Ishmael. (Genesis 25:12-18) The surprising thing about Iraq is that they are antiquity confronting our modern world. Here is an old Biblical nation although backed by Russia threatening modern man and his life line oil. Here is a real time tunnel, ancient Babylon's presence which reminds our present world of antiquity, and the plan of Bible prophecy decreed by God, such things must come to pass. (Rev. 1:1-4)

What Does Iraq's Aggression Mean?

The Bible presents the Gentiles of which Iraq is one nation as constantly in a state of rebellion against the God of heaven. Iraq as a people are a war like nation knowing only commitment to Communist revolutionary doctrine. Is the Iraqi aggression in Kuwait predicted in Scripture? We have already said no it is not foreshadowed in Scripture with any significance. While the Bible does not speak of such an event, yet it does speak of one king or country gobbling up another in end time events on God's Armageddon calendar.

Iraq echoes a message to us today that God has decreed or determined the course and outcome of our modern world. Whatever the Lord God has planned will be! (Ephesians 1:11) All the nations of the earth will mourn over Christ at his Second Coming. (Rev. 1:7) This will be the end of man's day and the beginning of God's day.

Will Iraq Continue To Attack Israel?

The real question and issue, I believe is that the Iraqi aggression is really indirect Russian aggression in the Middle East. The Russian bid through Iraq is also a test to the Western world to determine our readiness to a nuclear attack and a Russian commitment to Marxist-Lenin doctrine of world rule. The Scriptures teach clearly the attempt of Russia for world rule and domination in the end times. This has been the dream of many leaders throughout the ages to rule the world. (See Chapter 4)

Things Don't Just Happen?

Fate is not ruling but God is ruling! God is Sovereign, God is over all and through all and in all but He is not the All. (Ephesians 4:6)

Are Their Figures Like Saddam Hussein In The Bible?

Yes, the personality of Saddam Hussein foreshadows the type of personality which will emerge in the end time, the World Dictator (the Anti-Christ). A similar type of historical figure Antiochus Epiphanes is predicted in Daniel Chapter 8. Antiochus Epiphanes foreshadows the Anti-christ.

Saddam Hussein's need like that of an earlier Babylonian monarch before him Nebuchadnezzar is to put personal faith in Jesus Christ to save him. Nebuchadnezzar's testimony of his salvation in the book of Daniel chapter 4 testifies to his heart need of personal trust in Jesus Christ for salvation.

Iraq will line up with Russia politically and militarily to come against Israel during the middle of the tribulation period. This is due to their belief in the god of military might and the military state.

Chapter Seven Study Questions

1. Is Iraq to be found in the Bible?

2. What does the Bible say about Iraq?

3. What does Iraqi aggression mean?

4. Are their other figures in the Bible like Saddam Hussein?

5. Will Iraq attack Israel?

Challenge Questions

1. What Iraqi monarch figured predominantly in Bible times in the book of Daniel?

2. Who will Iraq be aligned with in the end times?

8
Perilous Times

"But know by experience Timothy that in the last days difficult times will come." (II Tim. 3:1)

Difficult times are reserved for the last days which began with Paul and Timothy and will continue until the Rapture of the Church.

The Rapture

The Lord Jesus taught the truth of the Rapture on the night in which he fulfilled the will of God. (John 14:3) This was the night of His betrayal and arrest prior to His trials, and crucifixion.

The Apostles Taught And Believed The Rapture

The Apostle John taught the believers ultimate sanctification would be at the appearing of Christ. (I Jn. 3:1-2) Peter who was in the Upper Room, received direct revelation about the Rapture in I Peter 1:7. Paul the Apostle was given much revelation about the glorious teaching of the catching away of the church. (I Corinthians 15:51-58; I Thess. 4:13-18 and 5:1-11; II Timothy 4:8; Titus 2:13)

What Is The Rapture?

The rapture or snatching away of the church is a new truth that was not revealed until the time of Christ and His apostles. It is not the truth of the resurrection, but that a generation will be translated into heaven without dying. In this sense, the rapture is called a mystery in I Cor. 15 that all shall not sleep but we shall all be changed with an instantaneous glorification. Although the 15th chapter of I Corinthians contains the declaration of the gospel and truth about the resurrection, yet the Rapture is introduced in I Cor. 15:51-58.

Christ Will Appear In The Air

"For the Lord Himself will descend from heaven with the command, by voice of Archangel and by trumpet of God; and the dead in Christ will be raised up first, then we the ones living the ones being left together with them, we will be caught up in clouds to meet the Lord in air and in this manner we will be always with the Lord." (I Thess. 4:16-17 Greek New Testament)

Being Caught Up In The Air

The truth of being caught up in the air at Christ's appearing before the beginning of the tribulation is a living hope for believers. The apostles expected the Lord's return to be imminent that is nothing need be done further on God's prophetic time clock. The Lord will appear suddenly without any warning and the redeemed blood bought believers from the formation of the church on the day of Pentecost until the rapture will be taken home to the Father's house.

The Church Will Not Go Through The Tribulation

"For God has not appointed us for wrath, but for obtaining salvation through our Lord Jesus Christ." (I Thess. 5:9) Salvation in this context is deliverance through the Lord Jesus at the rapture of the church. This is to be seen in contrast to being destined to go through the tribulation of wrath on the earth. The living or sleeping of I Thess. 5:10 are the one's translated at the Lord's return, (I Thess. 4:16-17).

Tribulation Comes Next

"When they cry peace and security then destruction will come upon them suddenly without any warning as labour pains upon a woman with child and they shall not escape." (I Thess. 5:3)

The Church Age

This period within the dispensation of Grace began on the Day of Pentecost and continues until the Rapture. (being caught up I Thess. 4:17) The church age will be characterized by Apostasy and Denials of the Truth. The Church Age will never end in a *Golden Age* as some have claimed through the years, and claim even today.

"For the mystery of lawlessness is already at work; only he who restrains will do so until he be taken out of the way." (II Thess. 2:7)

"Evil men and impostors will proceed from bad to worse deceiving and being deceived." (II Tim. 3:13)

"Let no one deceive you, for it will not come unless the apostasy comes first, and the man of lawlessness be revealed, the son of destruction." (II Thess. 2:3)

Things are not going to get better and better in our world but the Bible teaches they are going to get progressively worse ending with the revelation of the Man of Sin.

The Parables

The parables of Matthew 13 give the characteristics of this interim form of the kingdom of God. The Church age is only a part of this overall present eternal theocratic rule of God.

Parable Sower and Soils- A good sowing of the Word of God in the present form of the kingdom. (Mt. 13:1-9)

Parable of the Tares- A false sowing is to take place in the kingdom seen in the liberal church, social gospel and many sects and cults. A denial of the Deity of Jesus Christ and His substitutionary atonement on the cross is the heart of this false gospel sown in our world today. (Mt. 13:24-30) Jesus Christ is God of very God. He took the sinner's place on the cross. (I Cor 15:3) Yes, Christ died for sinners. He took their place on the cross. He died for me! Did die for you? Will you receive Christ as your savior?

Parable of the Mustard Seed- The kingdom will have an insignificant beginning but will continue until it is fully developed throughout the whole earth. (Mt. 13:31-32)

Parable of the Leaven- The present interim form of the kingdom will develop silently and steadily working like leaven until the kingdom is fully developed. (Mt. 13:33)

Parable of Hidden Treasure- The present form of the kingdom will include both Gentiles and Israel who will be hidden away throughout the world dispersed among the Gentiles. (Mt. 13:44-46)

Parable of Dragnet and of Fish- The present temporary form of the kingdom will end in judgment. (Mt. 13:47-50)

Unbelief

The present temporary form of the kingdom, of which the present church age is part, is characterized by unbelief. This response to truth is evidenced by religious liberals, clergymen who are liberals, moderates, and other continual denials of the truth of God. (II Peter 2:1) These false teachers so strongly presented in the Scripture are continually denying the Master (Despot) who bought them. They bring swift destruction upon themselves as Peter predicted and such began historically with Jude's day. (see the Epistle of Jude)

John the Apostle develops the theme of the false teacher in I John 4 and 5. The testimony of Christ abiding in the believer's life through the Holy Spirit is seen by the believer's testimony to the Lord.

I John 4:2 - "every spirit that confesses that Jesus Christ has come in the flesh is from God." Jesus was fully man and the reference is to the incarnation of our Lord. The Docetists taught Christ was a phantom having no body and this was a clever undercutting of the Substitutionary Atonement of Christ dying in the sinner's place.

I John 4:15 - "Whoever confesses that Jesus is the Son of God, God abides in him, and he in God." This is the individual's spirit testifying that Christ is the Son of God. He is God of very God, the eternal Son and second person of the triune God. The individual's assertion that Jesus is God will suffice and this will prove the Spirit's residence indwelling that person.

I John 5:1 - "Whoever believes that Jesus is the Christ is born of God; and whoever loves the Father loves the child born of Him." The point of this confession is to the Messiahship of Jesus Christ that He, Christ is prophet, priest and King.

Teacher Literacy

Why is it necessary to test the Teachers? John the Apostle was given the supervision of churches in the biblical Asia Minor which is modern Turkey. He wanted the elders in those churches to test travelling teachers by the three principles concerning the humanity, deity and Messiahship of Jesus. To test the teacher was to determine their right to speak in the Assembly. (I John 4:1) Those who did not confess the God-Man, Fully God & Fully Man and His Mission were not born of God. (born from above-no spiritual birth) They had not believed on Jesus as their Savior and had not been regenerated by the Spirit of God. Regeneration is the impartation of a new nature to the individual by the Spirit's indwelling and presence. (Titus 3:5-6)

The Spirit Of The Anti-Christ

"And every spirit that does not confess Jesus is not born of God; and this is the spirit of the Anti-Christ, of which you have heard that he comes, and now is already in the world." (I John 4:3)

Satan is the imitator of the things of God and John refers to Satan's imitation of Pentecost by his reference to the Spirit of Anti-Christ taking up his residence in the world.

Chapter Eight Study Questions

1. Where did the teaching of the doctrine of the Rapture originate?

2. Which Apostles believed the Rapture?

3. What is the meaning of the Rapture?

4. How will the Rapture occur?

5. Why doesn't the church go through the tribulation?

Challenge Questions

1. What is the relationship of the church age to the kingdom of God?

2. What do the parables tell us about the kingdom of God?

9
The Blessed Hope

The blessed hope is a term used by the Apostle Paul in Titus chapter 2 meaning the same as "being caught up." (I Thess. 4:17) The Latin word rapture means the same to snatch away. While the rapture is a truth taught in the Bible yet the word rapture is not used in the Scriptures but is referred to by these other synonymous inspired words. The references in the Bible to the appearing of Christ, the blessed hope, being caught up and the revelation of Jesus Christ communicate the truth taught in the bible of the Rapture.

The Rapture

The truth of the Rapture is our hope in everyday living that a generation will be translated and taken to heaven without experiencing physical death. (I Cor. 15:51-58) All of this will take place before the awful time of human suffering engulfs the earth known as the tribulation.

Jesus Taught It

"And if I go and prepare a place for you, I will come again, and receive you to myself; that where I am, there you will be." (John 14:3)

The Father's House

The translation of the church to heaven will be with the destination marked Father's House. "In my Father's house are many dwelling places; if it were not so I would have told you; for I go to prepare a place for you." (John 14:2) Keep on trusting the Father, keep on trusting in me." (John 14:1) Jesus claimed equality with the Father. He claimed to be God. Therefore, Christ asked us to believe in Him trust Him as our Savior and keep on resting and trusting in His death on the cross and His everyday sovereign control of all the earth.

Church In Heaven

The church is called the Bride of Christ in Scripture. We will be there to be rewarded for our service for Christ on the earth during our lifetime. The judgment seat of Christ or bema is the place where Christians earn a reward or suffer loss of reward. It has nothing to do with judgment because the believer trusting Christ as his Savior has been forgiven all transgressions at the cross. (Colossians 2:13c) The issue for the believer everyday on the earth is entirely different than for the non-Christian. For the believer having trusted Christ as Savior, the issue is to live his life in fellowship with the Father and His Eternal Son Jesus Christ, so that God's life, love and joy may be reproduced in His child on a daily basis. The issue for the non-Christian is their sin and condemnation, unless the trust Christ as their personal Savior. (Romans 8:1)

Judgment Seat Of Christ

The three major passages that refer to the truth of the bema for Christian following the Rapture of the Church are Romans 14:10, I Cor. 3:10-15, and II Cor. 5:9-11.

The Second Coming Of Christ

The second coming of Christ is an entirely different event and truth taught in the Bible than the Rapture. At the second coming, Christ comes to the earth to judge the earth. The Rapture of the church occurs seven years earlier than the Second Coming of Christ. The Second Coming of Christ occurs at the end of the seven year tribulation period. Matthew 24:29--Matthew 25:31 teaches the truth concerning the events of the Tribulation at the Second Coming of Christ.

John Believed The Rapture

"Believed, now we are children of God, and it has not appeared as yet what we shall be. We know that, when He (Christ) appears, we shall be like Him, because we shall see Him just as He is." (I John 3:2)

Peter Believed The Rapture

"That the proof of your faith, being more precious than gold which is perishable, even though tested by fire, may be found to result in praise and glory and honor at the Revelation of Jesus Christ." (I Peter 1:7)

Paul Believed And Taught The Rapture

"For the Lord Himself will descend from Heaven with the command relayed by the voice of the Archangel and the trumpet of God; and the dead in Christ will rise first. then we who are alive and remain shall be caught up together with them in the clouds to meet the Lord in the air, and thus we will always be with the Lord." (I Thess. 4:16-17)

"Looking for the blessed hope the appearing of the Glory of our great God and Savior, Christ Jesus." (TITUS 2:13)

"Behold, I tell you a mystery; we shall not all sleep, but

we shall all be changed. In a moment, in the twinkling of an eye, at the last trumpet; for the trumpet will sound, and the dead will be raised imperishable, and we shall be changed." (I Cor. 15:51-52)

The Church In Eternity

The Christian has a brighter hope after the Rapture of one day living in the *New Jerusalem.* Yes, the heavenly beautiful city is described so wondrously in Hebrews 12:22-24. (The good angels, the church those in Christ, the Lord Jesus, the Old Testament saints and the sprinkled blood.) The New Jerusalem, the eternal city will be suspended between heaven and earth. (Rev. 21:2) Read the twenty-first chapter of Revelation for an elaborate description of this city 1500 miles long, wide and high!

"Having the Glory of God. Her brilliance was as one brilliant jewel, as a stone of crystal-clear jasper." (Rev. 21:11)

Chapter Nine Study Questions

1. What is the meaning of the Blessed Hope?

2. Where will we be taken to following the Rapture?

3. What is the judgment seat of Christ?

4. What is the meaning of Hebrews 12:22-24?

5. What is our hope?

Challenge Questions

1. What is the meaning of Colossians 2:13c?

2. How does the Rapture differ from the Second Coming?

10
Hard Times

Perilous times began in Paul's day and continue down to the present time. (II Tim. 3:1) Economically, hard times come because of what men love and serve. The Bible predicts so clearly that in the last days men will be lovers of self, lovers of money, and lovers of pleasure to the exclusion of God. (II Tim. 3:2-4) Self love is normal the Bible teaches in Ephesians 5:29. The human obsession of self-love to self-worship and self-glorification is an end times spiritual and psychological sickness. This self love is seen in an obsession to make money and deification of the god of pleasure to the exclusion of the God of heaven. The NASB has the translation of "lovers of pleasure rather than God" but the Greek text given its full expression has to the exclusion of God. Modern man has an obsession in the last days with self, money and pleasure. Human suffering has to come because men are given over to these pursuits regardless of the human suffering of others.

This self worship cult is coupled with an outward ritualistic form of godliness. (II Tim. 3:5) The biblical psychology gives the true measure of man inwardly and outwardly. (II Tim. 3:1-9)

Bible prophecy gives me five further benefits spiritually, emotionally and psychologically that bring inner wellness and a healthy outlook on life. God's plan for the future is carefully, clearly and precisely recorded. Yes, you can completely trust the Bible it speaks without error in all of its entirety. Errors are recorded accurately. (John

1:45) Prophetic truth is reliable and a hundred percent trustworthy. (II Peter 1:16) Our need is to be established in the truth as Peter the Apostle established his readers in the truth of Christ's Second Coming. *I am clearly able to see the Western context what's ahead for me and my Western civilization with the Bible's presentation of the Armageddon Calendar and Context.*

The Spirit's ministry is a ministry in things to come that is the revelation of future things for the Church, Israel and also the Gentile nations of the world. (John 16:13) The faith, the body of revealed truth, the completed New Testament Canon was delivered once for all to the Saints around the end of the first century A.D. (up to 90 A.D.) (Jude vs. 3) The apostles received the New Testament Canon by direct revelation from God. The Apostle John received the book of the revelation of Jesus Christ, the last book, completing The New Testament Canon.

The Bible has as well a comforting effect on the human soul and spirit.

"Therefore comfort one another with these words." (I Thess. 4:18)

"Therefore comfort one another, and build one another up, just as also you do." (I Thess. 5:11)

Great blessings and peace of mind come from an accurate knowledge of the Bible applied to life. The conclusion can be drawn that Russia and China while end time world powers will never be world empires because God has not decreed it to go that way. A correct interpretation of Daniel 2 and 7 shows clearly these world powers decreed by God to be world empires, Babylon, Medio-Persia, Greece and Rome, the Revised Roman Empire and the Millennial Kingdom of Christ. (Oh and by the way, the European Economic Community is only a type of the Revised Roman Empire.)

The Bible is a treasury of great and precious promises given by God. (II Peter 1:4) The elative form of the adjective great is used to show that the promises are without comparison and their great value. The Bible uses the word precious only to speak of those things highly esteemed by God. The word precious is used also in reference to the Blood of Christ.

Western Context

II Timothy helps me to see the experience of Western civilization within the framework of the *Armageddon Calendar and Context*. The Bible predicts hard economic times for our world because of what men will be in the last days. This love of self, money, and pleasure will have neither regard for human suffering nor care who has to be stepped on to fulfill self, obtain money and pleasure. This is to be seen within the context of the Armageddon calendar and chronology of events. Hard economic times for the West intensify as the Western world enters the tribulation period, as the tribulation engulfs the earth.

The Communist world ends in the revelation of the Man of Sin, the Anti-Christ who worships the god of military might. (Daniel 11:38) The Western world weakened according to Ezekiel 38:13 with only a verbal rebuke (political rhetoric) to direct Russian aggression with all her allies against Israel. While love of self, money and pleasure has caused tremendous overspending in the Western world, the Communist world needs money and wealth every bit as much which explains their aggression into the Middle East. (Ezekiel 38:12)

Chapter Ten Study Questions

1. What is Western Civilization's experience in the Armageddon context?

2. What is the meaning of perilous times in II Timothy 3:1?

3. Why do hard times come?

4. Is man given to the pursuit of religion in the end times?

5. What does Peter the Apostle mean by the words great and precious promises? (II Peter 1:4)

Challenge Questions

1. What comparisons and contrasts can be drawn between East and West during this time?

2. What is the meaning of Ezekiel 38:12?

• • • • •

Religion
What is the end time religion?
How it determines your income?

11
The Beginning Of Religion

After the flood, the Lord God instituted the role of human government to help stop the lawlessness of the human heart. (Gen. 9:1-7) Man begins to rebel as illustrated by Nimrod. He was the one to institute the first religion the mother-child cult centering in the worship of his own wife and their son. Satan used Nimrod to set up a counter kingdom called Babel. The unifying feature of this false system of worship was the Tower of Babel. (Gen. 10:8-10; 11:1-9) The Lord God's judgment was seen in dividing them by causing each to speak a different human language not understandable to those outside their own language group. The religion of Nimrod, his wife and their son has been seen in every civilization and culture throughout the centuries in the form of the mother-child cult.

Babylon The Great

The book of Revelation develops the theme of the mother-child cult in the end time religion. (Revelation 17)

"And the woman was clothed in purple and scarlet, and adorned with gold and precious stones and pearls, having in her hand a gold chalice full of abominations and of the uncleanness of her fornication." (Revelation 17:4)

"And upon her forehead a name was written, a mystery, Babylon the great, the mother of harlots and of the abomination of the earth." (Revelation 17:5)

Who Is This Woman?

The identity of the woman is given in Revelation 17:9, the woman sits on seven mountains. Rome is the city long known to be built on seven mountains. (John F. Walvood, Revelation, Chicago: Moody press, pp. 250-251).

The false system of worship the mother child cult which began with Nimrod and the worship of his wife and son, seen throughout every civilization is with us today, in the form of the Mary-Jesus cult.

No Church In The Old Testament

The church announced as future by Jesus in Matthew 16 was formed on the Day of Pentecost. (Mt. 16:18; Acts 2:1-4; 11:15) The Spirit of God who was already in the world as seen beginning with Genesis 1 took up His residence and formed the church on the Day of Pentecost. Earlier, Jesus had predicted through the sowing of the good seed that the Word would go forth until His Second Advent at the end of the age. (Mt. 13:1-9)

The sons of Adam named Cain and Abel had been taught that the way of approach to a Holy God after the fall of their parents was on the basis of blood sacrifice. (Gen. 4) The acceptance of the principle of forgiveness of sin through the shedding of blood demonstrated their faith in the Coming Redeemer. (Gen. 3:15) Abel accepted the truth laid down for him but his brother rejected that way of salvation and presented a works principle trying to work his way to heaven. Abel's offering was accepted but Cain's offering was rejected by the Lord God. (Gen. 4:5)

The Reformation

The Reformers set straight the doctrine of Soteriology (salvation) beginning with Luther in the 1500's. Righteousness of God was appropriated through faith in Jesus Christ rather than through the church. (Romans 1:17; 3:22) The Reformers protested that the Church of

Rome was grossly in error on the doctrine of salvation. The Grace of God was dispensed only by Jesus Christ rather than the sacraments of the church then or now for that matter. The easy to understand Bible doctrine of the mediatorship of Jesus Christ is that there is only one God and one mediator between God and man the God-Man, Christ Jesus. (I Tim. 2:5)

The World Church

The parable of the tares told by Jesus in Matthew 13 predicts a false sowing of the seed, the doctrines and the traditions of men rather than the Word of God. (Mt. 13:24-30) This false sowing is carried out indirectly, by Satan through his servants. (II Corinthians 11:13-15)

The final form of this false sowing is the super church of all unregenerate peoples who do not believe the importance of the Bible's Salvation by grace nor the following of the teachings of the Bible. Doctrine is not important but rather our experience, unifying principles of religion, and our humanity. (II Timothy 4:3) The world council church seen in Revelation 17 is completely reabsorbed back into Rome. (17:3)

Religion Of Pleasure

The religion of man has been a religion and worship and pursuit of pleasure to the exclusion of God. (II Tim. 3:4) The true intent and motives of the human heart during the last days has been hidden by the worship and outward forms of ritualism of man's heart. (II Tim. 3:5)

The Anti-Christ Of Armageddon Calendar

The beast known to us as Anti-Christ was revealed by Divine permission at the beginning of the 7 year period of tribulation on the earth. (Rev. 6:2) More revelation is given to us in chapter 13 of this coming Gentile ruler who will

79

rule the World.

"And One from his heads as slain to death, and the heaven sent plague his death has been healed and the earth is whole (one) and the earth marvelled (that's supernatural - he's God) after the beast." (Greek New Testament - Rev. 13:3)

The Anti-christ's death wound is not his restoration to life from his own physical death. The death wound that is healed is the Anti-christ's ability to unify and revive the Roman Empire.

The earth worshiped the Anti-christ and the dragon. (Satan-Rev. 20:2) Satan gave his authority to the Anti-christ.

The False Prophet

The beast is a political world ruler who himself worships the god of military might. (Daniel 11:36) This totalitarian dictator has no respect for any human rights nor the sacredness of life in any form other than militarism. (Dan. 11:37-38) The false prophet is the religious spokesman for the beast who proclaims the deity of the first beast. (Rev. 13:12) The false prophet is able to perform great signs so that the hearts of those on the earth are deceived during the days of the tribulation. (Rev. 13:13) The religious prophet makes an image of his boss the beast and all the more astounding is that he gives life to the statue. (Rev. 13:15) He gives by divine permission breath to the image of beast which comes to life and speaks and names those who are to be executed because of their failure to worship the beast's statue. (Rev. 13:15)

Economics Is Tied To Religion

"And he (false prophet) provides that no one should be able to buy or sell except the one that has the mark of the beast either the number (666) or his name." (Rev. 13:17-18)

World Church Is Destroyed By Anti-Christ

The world church composed of Rome, the Liberal Protestant Church, all religions and cults except the blood bought Christian has forced a peace treaty upon Israel, at the beginning of the seven year period, bringing a comprehensive and everlasting peace plan to the region for 3 1/2 years. Now the Anti-Christ turns on the World Church centered in Rome to destroy it prior to the time of his own demand for worship. (Rev. 17:16-18)

The Final Form Of Worship

The final form of worship during the tribulation period is the worship of the Devil. Black magic or Satanism which is surfacing all over the earth at the present time and a threat to modern society is universally adhered to during the Tribulation period.

"And they worshiped the dragon, because he gave his authority to the beast;" (Revelation 13:4)

"And He (Jesus Christ) laid hold of the dragon, the serpent of old, who is the Devil and Satan, and bound him for a thousand years." (Revelation 20:2)

The transition is from the triumph though short lived of the world church at the beginning of the tribulation period to the worship of a man the Anti-Christ and then to Satanism. Communism is preparing the world, for the Anti-Christ; and the Marxist-Lenin doctrine is a religion though with revolutionary sacraments. Communism is the worship of man. Anti-Christ is Satan's man and the one whom Satan will present to the world and Israel as their Savior and Messiah. (Luke 4:6)

Good Sowing During The Tribulation

The ministry of the 144,000 Jewish Christian Evangelists takes place at the beginning of the 7 year tribulation period and continues throughout the entire period. (Rev. 7:1-8) The result of their ministry is pictured for us in Rev. 7:9-17. Those who responded to the message of the 144,000 which is directed at the Gentile world were put to death, and death was by being beheaded. (Rev. 7:9-17)

The ministry of the two witnesses referred to in great detail in Revelation 11 is to Israel as well as the Gentiles. They are carrying out their ministry from Jerusalem and that message is carried by the media throughout the whole earth. (Rev. 11:9) The two witnesses have the power to perform miracles and to protect themselves even to taking life from those who would harm them. (Revelation 11:5-6)

They are killed by Anti-Christ after completing their ministry. (Revelation 11:7) The dead bodies of these two messengers of God will lie in state for 3 1/2 days and the earth will refuse them a burial. (Rev. 11:9)

"And after three and a half days the spirit of life from God came into them, and they stood on their feet; and great fear fell upon those beholding them." (Revelation 11:11)

Chapter Eleven Study Questions

1. Where did religion begin?

2. What do the words Babylon the Great mean?

3. When did the Church begin?

4. What truth were the Reformers clarifying and defending?

5. What is the meaning of the parable of the tares?

Challenge Questions

1. Does religion determine income?

2. What is the end time Religion?

12
Iraq Is Communist Russian Brand

Iraq's aggression of Kuwait has nothing to do with it being a real part of the old Babylonian Empire. This was predicted by the Bible and well there you are folks. Nonsense! This is gross distortion and twisting of Bible passages to make the Bible say something that it does not say. The aggression of Saddam Hussein and his Communist Iraq has to do with the Red Revolution that was started with Lenin, other revolutionaries in Russia in 1917. Saddam is a committed Communist revolutionary in the same sense of other communist revolutionaries like Lenin.

Why Is Saddam Hussein Still On Top?

Why is Saddam Hussein still the head of rule and the party in Iraq? He is Russian backed and sponsored, and no doubt partly due to his own skill and cunning. Samir al-Khalil states emphatically in his earlier work *Republic Of Fear* published by UCLA press, Berkeley, 1989 on page 16: "In Saddam Hussein's reorganization, the boss became a faceless party bureaucrat."
The secret police emerged in Iraq their counterpart in Russia was the KGB. (Ibid, p. 20) Samir al-Khalil points out that Saddam's language is always that of the revolution. History points to the extensive April 1972 Iraq-Soviet Friendship. (Ibid, p. 316) In May 1972, Communists entered the Iraqi government for the first time. Saddam Hussein became President of Iraq in June 1979. In June

and July of the same year, mass execution of top Bathi command was carried out. As well, one third of the members of RCC (Revolutionary Command Council) were executed. (Ibid, p. 317) Some five hundred top-ranking Bathists are said to be executed as well. (p. 317) Hussein as head of Iraq removed any and all opposition to himself and the Revolution by execution. Yes, Hussein is the Stalin of Iraq. Iraq is Communist-Red Russian Communist brand. The Soviet Union may have changed their name to Russia but their doctrine hasn't changed. The Bible predicts a world power named Russia in end time events but does not know of a nation called the Soviet Union.

Iraq Explained

Present day aggression on the part of Iraq is easily explained by the fact that the Russian revolution which began in Russia in 1917, known as the Bolshevik Revolution, has spread to Iraq and with full Iraqi cooperation.

It is no less a pawn to see the present day Iraq as a rebuilding of part of the Old Babylonian Empire. Such is never predicted in Holy Writ! Scripture has to be tortured and twisted to say such and as for Saddam's rebuilding and the splendor of his kingdom compared to past monarchs as Nebuchadrezzar, well Communism thinks of everything! The false prophets of Jeremiah's day were equally duped and duped the masses with their message of all will be well. The bible student who has no Ph.D. may well interpret the phenomena of Iraq in such light. The explanation of Iraq, their Kuwait aggression, as a fulfillment of Scripture is not to be found in the Bible.

Babylon's Fall

Daniel predicted the fall of Babylon. The succession of world empires was decreed by God to be from Babylon to Medio-Persia. Daniel chapter 2 recounts the dream that the Babylonian king Nebuchadnezzar received. He saw an image and Daniel tells of that image:

"You O King, were looking and behold, there was a single great statue; that statue, which was large and of extraordinary splendor, was standing in front of you, and its appearance was awesome." (Dan. 2:31)

"The head of the image as gold, the breast and arms were silver, the belly and thighs bronze and legs iron, feet a mixture of iron and clay." (Dan. 2:32-33)

Nebuchadnezzar's Dream Interpreted

Daniel declared the interpretation beginning in Daniel 2:36:

"This....the dream; now we shall tell its interpretation before the king. Nebuchadrezzar, you are the head."

Yet notice with the progression of the interpretation in Daniel 2:39, the progression of power is from Babylon to Medio-Persia.

"And after you there will arise another kingdom inferior to you, then another third kingdom of bronze, which will rule over all the earth."

The world empire to arise to conquer Babylon was Medio-Persia. Cyrus the Persian conquered the Babylonian kingdom in 539 B.C. As to the fact that Babylon was never predicted to be rebuild nothing could be clearer than Isaiah 13:17-20 .

"Behold, I am going to stir up the Medes against them,.....and Babylon, the beauty of Kingdoms, the glory of the Chaldeans' pride will be as when God overthrew Sodom and Gomorrah. It will never be inhabited or lived in from generation to generation."

Communist Propaganda

The Hussein rebuilding of Iraq stems from in part no doubt the Iraqi pride of life and Saddam's egoism. The God of heaven has not decreed such nor is such a rebuilding and restoration of glory ever predicted to return to Iraq. It may well be a clever ploy to cover that Iraq is Red Russian Communist through and through. Russia thinks of everything! Eventually, the Bible predicts the triumph of Communism (the worship of man) in the form of the reign of the Coming world dictator. (the Anti-Christ) Jesus spoke of the coming time of deception so great on the earth that even the elect will be deceived. Friend, that time is here! (Mt. 24:4;24:24)

Chapter Twelve Study Questions

1. What kind of Communism is followed in Iraq?

2. What group is Saddam Hussein head of in the leadership in Iraq?

3. What influence did the Bolshevik revolution of 1917 have on Iraq?

4. What does the Bible teach about Babylon?

5. Is Babylon to be rebuilt? Why not?

Challenge Questions

1. How is Russian propaganda seen in modern day Iraq?

2. How is Matthew 24:4 and 24:24 to be understood?

• • • • •

The World Dictator
What do we know for sure concerning the beast?

13
The Dictator's Time

The beginning of his dictatorship starts with the making of the peace treaty for the Middle East region.

"And he will make a covenant with the many for seven (years)," (Daniel 9:27)

The dictator's rule will run the course of the entire seven year period ending with the Second Coming of Christ.

"And then that lawless one will be revealed whom the Lord Jesus will slay by the Spirit of His mouth and bring to an end by the appearance of His Coming." (2 Thess. 2:8)

The Little Horn

Scripture gives an elaborate description to the character of the Anti-Christ and his rule. He is called the little horn in Daniel (7:8), the King of Fierce Countenance (8:23), the Prince that shall come (9:26), and the desolator (9:27), the Vile Person (11:21), and the Wilful King (11:36).

The Beast

The Book of the Revelation gives the title of the BEAST to the Anti-Christ since from God's perspective that is exactly what he is. (Revelation 11:7, 13:1 and 17:8)

The Political Machine

The Anti-Christ is called a blasphemer of God, heaven, Christians and miraculous events such as the Rapture. (Revelation 13:6) He is backed by the rhetoric of a religious figure, the false prophet, and the power and authority of Satan. (Revelation 13:4; 13:11-18) He has a group of ten countries behind him who have been conquered by him or have willingly accepted his rule. (Daniel 7:23-24; Revelation 13:1)

Economical Control

The religious figure the false prophet will regulate the world's economy in that without the number or mark of the world dictator, it will not be possible to earn a living. At this point in the history of the earth during the tribulation period, the separation of church and state disappears. (Rev. 13:16-17)

Declared To Be God

The first 3 1/2 years of the Dictator's reign is characterized by peace for the Middle East region and for Israel. Ezekiel pictures Israel dwelling at peace without any need of protection just prior to a direct attack and intervention by Russia in the Middle East region. The Dictator by divine predestination, God moved on him, removed Israel's security prior to the time of the Russian attack. Then the Anti-Christ moves his headquarters to the Holy Land and proclaims Himself as God. (Ezekiel 38-39; Daniel 11:45)

Anti-Semitism Reigns In The Middle East

Anti-Christ persecutes Israel for the next 3 1/2 years in a terrible Jewish purge predicted by Jesus in Matthew 24:15-28.

This intense persecution of the Jew is due to the

Satanic hatred of the chosen nation. (Revelation 12)

Tribulation Christians Martyred

Those who become Christians during the Tribulation period whether as the result of the ministry of the 144,000 or the 2 witnesses will be put to death for their trust of Christ as their Savior. (Revelation 6:9-11)

Anti-Christ Destroyed By Jesus

The reign of Anti-Christ will be terminated by a direct judgment from God. The books of Ezekiel, Daniel and Revelation teach and support this truth. (Daniel 7:9-12; 7:22,26; 8:25; 11:45; Rev. 19:19-20). Anti-Christ will be cast into the lake of fire. (Rev. 19:20)

Who Is The Anti-Christ?

A great deal of speculation has taken place in the past trying to determine his identity. Many have thought during particular periods of time that Mussolini, or Hitler, were the Anti-Christ. Others have thought that the Pope was the AntiChrist. Throughout the history of the centuries following the cross, others have taken the Greek numerical value for the name of the individual candidate by assigning that value to each letter in the individual's name. All such endeavors are based on speculation. Frankly, we do not know who the Anti-Christ is at this point in time.

When Will Anti-Christ Be Revealed?

The Anti-Christ will be revealed following the Rapture of the church. (II Thessalonians 2:8) The Savior and the Apostles taught a number of mysteries one of which was given to Paul in II Thessalonians. The mystery of lawlessness is already at work, as it was in Paul the Apostle's day and continues until the falling away, and the Rapture of the church, and ends in the revelation of the Man of Sin.

II Thessalonians 2:8 confirms that the reign of Anti-Christ will be after that of his master Satan with miracles, signs, and false wonders. The same context tells us that he will use all possible deception and wickedness at his disposal to carry out his duration of office.

The earth because they loved the pleasure of unrighteousness will believe the lie that this ruler is God. (2 Thess. 2:10-12)

Chapter Thirteen Study Questions

1. What do we know of the Beast's political reign?

2. Is the world economy tied to the worship of the political figure?

3. What religious activities does the Beast and the false prophet engage in?

4. What is the end of the beasts?

5. When will Anti-Christ be revealed?

Challenge Questions

1. What direction does the political machine of the beast take?

2. What does The Prophet say about the political beast?

• • • • •

Chronology
What is coming?
Can't you feel it?

14
What Is To Come?
Events Prior to Armageddon Calendar

1. The continual cry of individuals and nations for peace and security intensifies until tribulation engulfs the earth. (I Thess. 5:1-11)

2. Unrest continues with upheavals in the Middle East from time to time. (Psalm 2)

3. Crime spreads. (II Thess. 2:7)

4. The Rapture of the church occurs prior to the beginning of the Tribulation. (John 14:1-3; I Cor. 15:51-58; I Thess. 4:13-18)

God's Prophecy Clock Begins to Tick

5. World Dictator, the Man of Sin, begins his rule on the earth. (II Thess. 2:3)

6. World Church Unites with Dictator (Rev. 17:3)

7. Peace Treaty Enforced (Daniel 9:27)

8. Dictator's Installation Service (Daniel 9:26-27; Rev. 17:3-5)

9. Dictator Destroys World Church-Thousands Killed (Rev. 17:16-18)

10. The Prophet Supports Dictator (Rev. 13:11-18)

11. Deception Epidemic Scale (Mt. 24:23-26; II Thess. 2:11-12; Rev. 13:15)

12. Israel Persecuted (Dan,. 9:27; Mt. 24:15; Luke 19:42; I Thess. 5:11)

13. God's Judgments seals-trumpets-bowls (Revelation 6-19)

14. Earthquake! (Rev. 6:12-16)

Three and Half Years Later

15. War In The Middle East- Desert Storm II Russia and Allies Attack Israel (Ezekiel 38-39)

16. Dictator Moves Headquarters-Update Jerusalem (Daniel 11:45)

17. Dictator Declares War (Daniel 11:41-43)

18. Prophet Proclaims Dictator is God (Daniel 11:36-39; Rev.13:12)

19. Desert Storm III-Egypt and Russia Attack Dictator (Dan.11:40)

20. Orient Attacks- Army Human Wave (Rev. 9:16)

21. Strange Object Appears In Sky (Mt. 24:30)

22. Christ Comes Back (Mt. 24:30)

23. Armageddon- God's Day (Mt. 24:31)

24. Israeli Head Count (Mt. 24:31)

25. Gentiles Lose Power - Times of Gentiles End (Mt. 25:31-46)

26. Millennial Kingdom - Jesus Rules from Jerusalem-The Nations Worship (Isaiah 2)

Chapter Fourteen Study Question

1. What continuous signs occur prior to the Rapture?

2. When will God's prophetic time clock begin to tick?

3. What are 6 facts that the Bible teaches about the world dictator and the reign of the false prophet?

4. What events occur during the last 3 1/2 years of the 7 year period known as the Tribulation?

5. How is Revelation 17:3-5 to be understood?

Challenge Questions

1. Where does the dictator move his headquarters?

2. What does the Scripture teach about the religious deception of the tribulation period?

Help small business 202-205-6523
202-720-1490

FOR migranT-$ ore 503-2452600 - 245-2600
hiring wash 509 248-6751
hiring

I want to START a business, but have no money
425-743-9469 541-924-8480
oregon
206-447-9224
206-323-0534